When Silence Speaks

When Silence Speaks

The Life and Spirituality of Elisabeth Leseur

Jennifer Moorcroft

Gracewing

First published in 2019 by
Gracewing
2 Southern Avenue
Leominster
Herefordshire HR6 0QF
United Kingdom
www.gracewing.co.uk

No part of this publication may be reproduced, stored in a retrieval system, or transmitted in any form or by any means, electronic, mechanical, photocopying, recording or otherwise, without the written permission of the publisher.

The rights of Jennifer Moorcroft to be identified as the author of this work have been asserted in accordance with the Copyright, Designs and Patents Act 1988.

© 2019 Jennifer Moorcroft

ISBN 978 085244 903 5

Typeset by Gracewing

Cover design by Bernardita Peña Hurtado

CONTENTS

Introduction..vii

1 Early Life..1

2 Marriage..15

3 Conversion..29

4 Confronting Unbelief..45

5 Work Among the Poor..65

6 Juliette..85

7 Treatises for Her Nephew and Niece......................97

8 Apostolate of Prayer..109

9 A Soul Sister..123

10 Suffering Accepted and Offered..........................135

11 Félix's Conversion..153

12 The Priesthood..169

Bibliography..181

Introduction

'THE CHRISTIAN LIFE is great and beautiful and full of joy', wrote Elisabeth Leseur. I have written several books on saints, and my purpose in all of them was to show through their lives the truth of this. One of the greatest exemplars of the beauty and joy of the Christian life was Elisabeth herself. As one of her friends said of her, 'Some beings are a light toward which all turn who need light to live by'.

She has a special place because she was a lay woman who became holy in a secular milieu, concerned with the issues of her day which, although those of a century or more ago, are of just as much concern today. She was involved in the beginnings of the feminist movement and brought to the issues her own understanding of a woman's role in society. She was deeply involved with various social initiatives of her day. She lived in a milieu of militant atheism and pondered deeply what her response to it should be. Suffering from ill health for most of her life, perhaps her greatest contribution to our era where euthanasia is increasingly seen as the best response to pain, she draws on her Catholic faith to demonstrate a deeply moving and shining alternative.

Because of the illnesses from which she suffered throughout her life, to her great sorrow she was unable to have children of her own. Far from her childlessness making her turn in upon herself, she made her great maternal instincts into a power for good, in her love for her family and their children, whom she loved as her own, but also in her untiring work among the poorest in her society, especially the children. She can thus be a great example to those who, like her, remain childless.

Elisabeth came from a conventional Catholic family but found that a conventional Christian life was not strong enough to withstand the challenge of atheism. Her husband, Félix, asked what was it that changed a conventional Catholic into someone who lived her faith to an outstanding and heroic degree. Her conversion came when she understood that she had to live her Catholic life in depth, with the commitment of her whole life, if she were to respond to the atheistic milieu in which she found herself and to understand deeply the faith that she considered was its only answer. It also provided the only answer to the sorrows of bereavement in her life, and the meaning of her own sufferings of mind and body. It was the beginning of a great adventure.

She was an incomparable friend and a prolific letter writer to her friends and family. Félix remarked on the beauty of her style; she was able to express herself with great clarity and humility and had undoubted gifts of writing. Since she was unable to speak openly of her faith in the presence of unbelievers, the fact that she was able to write to her friends and family, sharing their problems, their joys and their grief, was a consolation to her and an avenue that God opened to her and to subsequent readers. Only to Sr Goby, though, was she able to share the depths of her faith with one who was following the same path.

No less remarkable was the journey of her husband, from his upbringing in a fervent Catholic family to militant atheist and then, after Elisabeth's death, to conversion and ordination as a Dominican priest. Although Elisabeth was given an inner assurance of this during her lifetime, the journey was accomplished only after her death and surely this is fortuitous. Central to her spirituality was the doctrine of the Communion of Saints, where all people of good will, past present and future, are united in the bond of love of the Trinity itself. From her place in heaven, Elisabeth's prayers guided her husband from unbelief to the return of his faith; it is a vibrant witness to the power of prayer and the assurance that this life, contrary to what Félix believed as an atheist, was not the end.

Whenever there is an English translation available I have used that. I am grateful to my husband, David, for checking my translations from the French, but any errors in them are mine alone.

I am grateful for the encouragement I have received from Joanne Mosley and the late Fr Tom of *Mount Carmel* magazine, who have supported me in all my writing. My thanks go, also, to Michael Burney, of the Elisabeth Leseur Society, for his help, advice and encouragement. I am grateful, also, to Rachel Edney, who kindly proofread the text and made invaluable suggestions. My thanks, too, to Jennifer McNeil, who with her husband have launched a new website, elcause.org, promoting her Cause, and who have also provided much encouragement.

Happily, Elisabeth's Diary, in various editions, is continually in print. Her husband amassed over 2,000 letters, only a selection of which have been published in French, and even fewer translated into English. Janet Ruffing has done a great service by editing the French edition of the letters between Sr Goby and Elisabeth. With the Cause of her beatification continuing, it is to be hoped that more of her letters will see the light of day in English and do as much good to those who read them today as they did to their original recipients.

1

EARLY LIFE

ELISABETH LESEUR WAS born into privilege. Her parents were of a middle class and wealthy professional background that gave her a comfortable existence; far more than this, they gave her the ability to develop her great gifts of intellect and mind within a happy and stable family life.

Her father, Antoine Arrighi, was from a wealthy Corsican family; he came to Paris to complete his law studies and obtained a doctorate in law, something that was rare at that time. He was esteemed for his brilliant intellect but even more for his integrity, his goodness and charm. This, combined with his hard work, gave him easy entry into the Paris bar, so once he had completed his studies, he settled down in Paris to pursue his career there, rather than returning to his native Corsica. He never forgot his origins though, and in 1867 was elected to the General Council of Corsica.

Elisabeth's mother, Marie-Laure (Gatienne) Picard, was the daughter of her father's second marriage. After his first wife died, her father, François Picard, married Elisabeth-Barthélemy Doras-David 12 December 1829, and Marie-Laure was born 30 December 1842, the last of the four children to be born from this marriage. M Picard had a brilliant career in the Ministry of Finance and died in February 1862, when Gatienne was only nineteen; her unmarried uncle, Alexandre Doras-David, moved in with the family as their surrogate father. He, too, was a minister in the French Government's Ministry of Finance, and was also an accomplished amateur violinist. One of his friends was Rossini, with whom he played the violin. He developed a love for music in Gatienne; she had a genuine talent for the piano and passed that love on to her children. Antoine and Gatienne married on 27 November 1865 at Saint-Roch in Paris, which would be the family's first parish.

The Arrighis had an apartment on the rue Baillif in Paris, which no longer exists, now swallowed up by the Bank of France, which at that time was near their apartment, and its name changed to rue Colonel-Driant. It was here that Elisabeth was born, 16 October 1866. At the time, her father was thirty years old and her mother twenty three. Gatienne was a worthy match for her older husband, being cultivated, intelligent and passionate.

Their parents went on to have four more children. Amélie was born 4 September 1868, the only boy, Pierre, 13 August 1870. Juliette was born two years later, 5 September 1872 and Marie, the youngest, was born 18 March 1875. All the children were highly intelligent, with Pierre eventually following his father into practising law.

No account of the family would be complete without mentioning Marguerite (Mamie) Drouillat, their much loved servant, described as hardworking, honest and kind, and who was treated as one of the family. She brought up all the Arrighi children and was as fond of them as they were of her; but she called Elisabeth 'my great love'. Many of Mamie's relatives also worked for the Arrighis and later for Elisabeth when she set up her own home.

With their expanding family the Arrighis moved several times before settling into an apartment in the rue du Rennes. They lived on the third floor and on the floor above them lived their widowed aunt, Mme Amélie Villetard de Prunières, their mother's much loved and lively elder sister, who was doted on by all the children. Her only son, Maurice, was eight years older than Elisabeth and was like an elder brother to her. Every Sunday the two families would dine alternately with each other.

On the fifth floor lived the Le Gros family, whose daughter, Yvonne, was a great and life-long friend to Elisabeth, and was like another sister to all the Arrighi children. So the apartment was almost like a commune, with all the families enjoying each other's company.

As well as the Paris apartment, the family owned a country house in Auteuil where they would spend several months during the spring and summer. A hamlet built between the thirteenth and seventeenth centuries, it became a fashionable country retreat for the French elite during the reign of Louis XV, once home to Victor Hugo and Molière and the birthplace of Marcel Proust. The area was, and is, commonly known as one of the richest in Paris, with calm, select and very expensive neighbourhoods. Elisabeth always preferred the country to the city and looked forward to staying there, with its rustic charm, its trees and flowers and lush gardens.

They had other children to play with, for the Chauvin family, who lived there, were close friends of the Arrighis. Mme Chauvin was called 'Tante Nancy' and their daughter, Louise, was one of Elisabeth's best friends. Louise and their son, also Pierre, were like brother and sister to the Arrighi children. Another family was the Lamberts, whose father was an advocate at the Paris Court with M Arrighi.

It was a delightful time for the families. It was close enough for the fathers to return from their offices in the evening, and all the families would enjoy eating out in their gardens when the weather was fine; very much a Parisian custom, painted famously by Monet.

All the children were initially taught at home, their first tutor being a Mlle Lœillot, until she left to get married to become Mme de Ville de Mirmont. On their return from

Auteil in 1877 the children had new teachers, the de Mas sisters, Louise and Amélie, whose well-to-do family had fallen on hard times; the two sisters became teachers to provide themselves with security in their retirement.

They were excellent teachers, Louise concentrating on music and the piano, which Elisabeth loved, and Amélie teaching such subjects as foreign languages, painting, history, geography and mathematics.

From that time on we know quite a bit about Elisabeth's childhood, because when they returned from Auteuil where Elisabeth had her eleventh birthday she began keeping a diary in a second notebook. There were three of these notebooks in all, but the first one is not extant. She began writing it with the encouragement of her mother and in preparation for her First Communion two years later. Besides chronicling her progress towards that day, they provide a lively portrait of the Arrighi family life.

Elisabeth began her diary with her happiness at the thought that she would be resuming her catechism classes on their return to Paris. The classes were given by the Abbé Séguin, parish priest of their parish church of Saint-Germain-des-Prés, which was in the same street as their apartment. Their father was by now a nominal Catholic, attending Mass with the family only on special occasions, and with no religious commitment. It was their mother who taught the children their first steps in the faith, teaching them their prayers, how to make the sign of the cross and going with them to Mass. She was a fervent Catholic, and took a great interest in preparing Elisabeth for her First Communion, sometimes going with her to the catechism classes and overseeing her homework afterwards. Besides her diary, Elisabeth also made detailed summaries on what they were being taught, and her reflections on it.

Early Life

The subjects covered concepts daunting to modern minds, especially when they were meant for eleven-year-old children—death, mortal and venial sin, hell and heaven. However, the subject of death had great relevance to people in the nineteenth century, when many children, even of the high bourgeoisie, died in infancy due to lack of hygiene and sanitation. One such child was a little girl in Elisabeth's catechism class, Eugénie Rocques, who made her First Communion early because she was terminally ill; she died only a few days before the rest of the class made their First Communion, while they were on retreat preparing for their great day. Then, only two months after starting her classes, Elisabeth heard the sad news of the death of the father of the de Mas sisters, and attended his funeral Mass. No doubt drawing on what she had learnt in her catechism class she reflected in her diary:

> Yes, death is a terrible thing, a cruel separation from those we love, but then what joy will they not have who will find again the beloved ones whom they have lost; one must be prepared for death, one should always seek to improve, to adorn the soul and not the body, because the soul will appear before God and what will not be the shame of sinners, to see that they have profited so little from the graces God had granted them.[1]

One can hear here more the solemn voice of their priest giving them instruction rather than that of Elisabeth, but it was no less heartfelt for that. She was both awed and repulsed by the thought of hell, but captivated by the far greater thought of receiving her Lord into her heart, and the thought of heaven. Meditating on this one day, she was so enraptured that she cried out, 'My God! Heaven!' Mamie came into the room at that moment and thought Elisabeth was rehearsing for a play. Elisabeth said, no, she wasn't, without revealing what was really happening, but she also noted in her diary that she was not sure that Mamie believed her.

The diary gives a picture of a lively, strong-willed and intelligent girl who was only too aware of her faults, the most important being her 'spirit of contradiction', her unwillingness to admit when she was in the wrong and her proclivity to being a tease. She was happy, then, when the catechism classes began, and M Séguin told them that they would be making their first Confession, for, as she said, 'I have great need of it!' Towards the end of November, on a Monday morning, Elisabeth, with her mother, went to the parish priest and while Elisabeth made her confession her mother went away for a short time. Elisabeth found it a very moving experience, and, as she put it, was not in the least intimidated.

It seems that her brother, Pierre, was the main butt of her teasing and quarrelling. Elisabeth confesses the times she had scraps and fights with her brother, and her fault in failing to live up to her good intentions of being more loving towards him, but she does not record how far she was provoked by Pierre into retaliation.

'I was naughty yesterday, a Sunday!' she recorded in her diary, 'I quarrelled with Pierre. Oh, it's horrible being eleven years old,' but she added that she knew the good God would forgive her because she afterwards apologised to him.[2]

In June, a prize-giving ceremony took place for the catechism class, with Elisabeth delighted to receive the prize of honour. She managed to keep back some impatience she felt towards her little sister Marie, thus keeping her good resolutions of the morning, but she was not at all happy when she was obliged to let the curate, M Sobaux, see her diary, feeling that it was only between her mother and God to see it. She had been upset on a previous occasion when her sister Amélie, that 'little Miss curiosity', wanted to see her diary: 'To punish her, I wouldn't give it to her; that is to say, I'm going to give it to Miss Curiosity to see, saying it was just for a laugh'.[3]

Her mother hadn't been feeling well, and Juliette also had been ill so the two of them went away for a month in July, taking Pierre with them as well. Elisabeth missed her beloved mother dreadfully, counting the days to her return. As the date of their return drew near, the rest of the family made bunting to put out to greet their arrival, and Elisabeth busied herself making a crocheted purse for her mother and toys for Pierre and Juliette. An even better present for her mother awaited her, because she would find her daughter completely changed, as Elisabeth confided to her diary:

> I am very kind at the moment; my dear little mother, when you return, you will no longer find a little girl teasing and full of self-love, no, but a little girl ready to give way in everything, very gentle and very kind; everything seems easy to me, now Mlle de Mas is very content with me.[4]

Maybe this transformation was because Pierre was not around for her to tease and quarrel with, because such a state of affairs was very short-lived. 'I was very nice yesterday' she was soon writing, 'although I still didn't want to give in to Pierre once, but afterwards I was nice'.[5]

She battled courageously against her faults, but as she remarked ruefully, although she made good resolutions she inevitably fell short of them. However, noting the number of times she recorded when she was naughty over a period of three and a half years, it is remarkable how few times she in fact fell short of her high standards.

In her diary Elisabeth mentioned more and more her longing to receive Holy Communion, and at last the great day had nearly arrived, preceded by a three-day retreat. Elisabeth wrote a detailed account of it, revelling in the time she was able to spend in church:

> How good this retreat is, above all because we can be in church, we sing, we pray, we meditate, we are wholly focused on the good God; but, at home, I have made myself a little altar where I pray and read. I enjoy this solitude, alone with the good God.[6]

This passage is very revealing, because it shows how far her spiritual life had already developed. She was able, even as a twelve year old, to remain at peace in the presence of God; she makes the distinction between vocal prayer and the meditation to which it should lead. She had also made a little private space where she could be alone, in a lively household, to be with God.

Even during the retreat, though, she had to confess that she had teased Amélie and hadn't been very kind to her:

> My mother asked me to look for something, and I told Amélie I would hold the candle. Amélie wanted to hold it but I wouldn't let her, so she went to tell mother, who said it was very bad of me to do that when I'm on retreat. I was full of remorse and from the bottom of my heart asked the good God to forgive me. That was very bad. And then I felt bad for my little mother who is so good. Still, I love her so much and I would like to please her, but I always fall down. I'm not nice.[7]

It was this delicacy of conscience that made her want to overcome herself, when such small incidents could cause her such grief. The following day all the children received absolution, so she could go forward to receive Jesus with a clear conscience. Then, on 18 May, as she received the Sacred Host for the first time:

Early Life

> It is over! The beautiful day of my First Communion has passed ... How can I express the bliss I tasted at that moment! I possessed Our Lord, he was in me, I was no longer alone, I was with Our Lord ... Yes, the day of First Communion is truly the most beautiful day in life.[8]

The following day she received Confirmation, 'and now all these joys are over. But I really hope I can renew them often'.[9]

Life returned to normal; her mother spent most of July away, there were lessons with the de Mas sisters, trips out to the theatre and visits to make. When the de Mas sisters opened classes in the rue du Mail at this time, the Arrighi girls then went there for lessons instead of at home. Mlle Louise said that Elisabeth worked hard at subjects that interested her; her liveliness, intelligence and amazing memory, something she inherited from her mother, made up for her lack of application in the rest. Elisabeth noted in her diary that she had been given some homework, to write two essays, one on natural history, and another on spelling, and that she preferred history and geography to French grammar, which gives a glimpse into her school work, and where her interests lay.

The whole milieu of the Arrighi family also gave her an invaluable education. Their parents arranged for trips out to the nearby Bois de Boulogne, to Saint-Cloud, to the theatre to see plays. Besides their regular holidays at Auteuil, they went to various places in France and Switzerland. Then, as Elisabeth grew older, she would be drawn into the company of the many influential people who were entertained at the Arrighi home.

Their uncle Alexandre, their mother's brother, courageous, loyal and kind, was of course always a welcome visitor, and he introduced his great friend, Auguste Louvrier de Lajolais to the family, who became a sort of uncle by adoption, and his wife a quasi aunt. He was a great promoter of the arts and, with a talent for organisation, set up many art exhibitions and expositions.

There were the Chaignets; M Chaignets occupied the chair of Letters at Poitiers University and was a correspondent of the Academy of Moral Science, an expert on the Greek philosophers Plato, Aristotle and Pythagorus, but possessing a great deal of humour and fantasy, which would have pleased the children.

Mme Massieu was an intrepid explorer, exploring the most difficult places of Asia, such as Tibet, Nepal, the valleys of the Irrawaddy and the Mekong, China and Mongolia. Again, she would have fired the imagination of the children, and Elisabeth, especially, would later become an inveterate traveller.

On the artistic side there were their close friends the Halévys, Louis Halévy the poet and man of letters, his sister-in-law Fromental, a celebrated musician and Ludovic, a member of the Académie Française. These were just a few of the people who made of the Arrighi household such an exciting and enlivening milieu in which to grow up.

With so many people of intellect and ability as frequent visitors to the Arrighi household, it is unsurprising that Elisabeth grew up during her teens to have a keen interest in everything that was happening in the outside world. Besides her studies with the de Mas sisters, which continued until she was seventeen or eighteen, her mother was also training her in the responsibilities that would be hers once she married and had a household of her own. She would be expected to be host to these friends who would also be coming to her house when that day arrived. As she moved into her teens this was not something in which Elisabeth was too interested; she notes in her diary that:

> My God, how bad I am! I wasn't kind yesterday evening. Me, I never think about what I'm doing, I'm preoccupied with knowing what's best for me, if it will be useful. I never look to talk, to be amiable and, if Mother makes observations, I show impatience and bad temper. Oh! It's so bad to be like that! I really would like to correct myself, but it is so difficult. I am making a resolution to do what I can to change and ask the good God to help me. I will pay attention to everything that's going on around me, I will talk, I will be pleasant. My God, help me, I pray; Saint Mary, pray for me.[10]

However many resolutions she was making, she still did not please her mother who took her aside one day and spoke sternly to her about her behaviour, the way she wasn't taking her studies seriously enough and not helping enough in the house:

> She told me that it was about time that I worked seriously, that every day I should take just one thing but do it very regularly and, when I forget to do it, I should write it in my diary since, once I get into the habit of doing one thing I can then take on something else to do.
>
> I'm making the resolution: I'm going to ask Mother to tell me what thing I should do. I will try to do it every day and, if I fail, I will write it in my diary and try to do better another time.[11]

She was as good as her word, and noted down every time she failed during that month of September. She finally stopped writing in her diary in March 1881. Her efforts were paying off, and she was beginning to blossom into the lovely young girl her mother—and she—wanted. However, her entry into womanhood was scarred by two events that would have lasting consequences. Staying in

Saint-Aubin in 1887 she became seriously ill with typhoid fever. This was not the only serious illness she had had, because during her childhood she had contracted hepatitis, which from then on would flare up from time to time. She recovered from the typhoid, but both illnesses would have repercussions throughout her life.

Then her youngest sister, the charming and gentle Marie who was only twelve years old and who had made her First Communion only two months earlier, also contracted typhoid, and died on the 5 July. As Elisabeth was to write later:

> She closed her beautiful eyes, full of tenderness, on the vision of things that pass, and opened her soul completely to the vision and the possession of that which lasts eternally.[12]

The enormous void Marie's death left in that close-knit family could be partially alleviated by their strong Christian faith, but her passing still left a raw and agonising pain in their hearts. As Elisabeth wrote a month later to a friend, also called Marie:

> You know how much affection I have for you and so it takes all my courage to write to you today. In thinking of you, I have to remember that last time we spent together, for us a complete happiness that we had enjoyed until then. It is only a month since then, we were united, happy, in good health, and today we are in Mussey, aunt is in Paris, and our dear little Marie is in heaven ... this is hard, very hard for us who were so united, and so I am not ungrateful to God, for we have immense consolations.

> Nothing was more peaceful, more gentle than the departure of that little soul; she slipped away without suffering into the arms of the good God.

> At the last moment she opened her eyes with a smile that remained after her death.[13]

Elisabeth told her how beautiful her little sister looked, dressed in the veil she had worn for her First—and last—Holy Communion. An added suffering was that they were not allowed to say goodbye to her before her death for fear of being infected with the dread disease. They left Paris shortly after the funeral to stay with a friend, Mme Duboys, to escape 'the noise that is so odious to us' as she put it, and to recover a little from their loss.

They had the consolation of knowing she was now in heaven, their tears more for themselves and their loss than for her. Elisabeth never recovered from the death of her beloved sister, but it became one brick in the foundation of her profound belief in the Communion of Saints.

Notes

[1] E. Leseur, *Journal d'enfant* (Paris: Editions du Cerf, 2012), p. 28.
[2] *Ibid.*, p. 32.
[3] *Ibid.*, p. 33.
[4] *Ibid.*, p. 44.
[5] *Ibid.*, p. 56.
[6] *Ibid.*, pp. 81ff.
[7] *Ibid.*, p. 85.
[8] *Ibid.*, p. 94.
[9] *Ibid.*, pp. 97ff.
[10] *Ibid.*, pp. 99ff.
[11] *Ibid.*, p. 100.
[12] R. P. M-A Leseur (Felix Leseur), *Vie d'Elisabeth Leseur* (Paris: J. de Gigord, 1946), p. 85.
[13] *Ibid.*, p. 86.

2

MARRIAGE

THE GAVIGNOTS WERE close friends of the Arrighi family, and they had stayed with them for a while in the rue Richelieu until they moved into their own house on the rue de Rennes. Like Elisabeth's father, M Gavignot was also a solicitor at the Court of Appeal and because of his work in legal circles they were also friends with M Leseur, who was an advocate at the Rheims tribunal. When, therefore, their younger son, Félix, wanted to pursue his studies at the Faculty of Medicine in Paris, M Leseur wrote to the Gavignots asking them to take him under their wing. He became almost a son of the family, dining with them regularly both when they were in Paris, and when they were at Passy in the summer.

Since the Arrighis were also such close friends of the family, it was only a matter of time before Elisabeth and Félix would meet each other at the Gavignots; this occurred one evening. Mme Gavignot said that the chemistry between the two was so immediate, so electric, that the whole room felt it. At the time Elisabeth had just turned 21 and Félix was five years older. Félix recalled that his first impression of her was that she was physically very charming, very agreeable, very distinguished in her bearing and her ways. Talking to her, Félix found that she was also cultured and that her mind was open to everything, with an intelligence that was remarkably quick and penetrating. She was especially interested in the arts, in literature and music. He was immediately drawn to her by her vivacity and her joyousness, with a beautiful laugh that rang out readily.

They soon found that they had a great deal in common, and Elisabeth's sister Amélie remarked that 'they are so boring; they talk about Wagner all the time!'

In the Spring of 1889 they revealed to their parents their attachment to each other, who were equally delighted with the match. The Leseurs were deeply Catholic and Elisabeth soon found herself at one with both his mother and his sister Claire, who were very involved in the Society of St Vincent de Paul and its social initiatives among the poor. M Leseur found in Elisabeth another dearly loved daughter.

Félix also found himself very much at home among the Arrighi family and their extended friends and relations. He had many conversations with their uncle Alexandre, who was a great help to him with his various projects.

The Leseurs gave him permission to escort their daughter to soirées and balls and the two met frequently to talk with each other. Amélie noted of the soirée of Saturday 18 May that it 'passed very agreeably. Elisabeth and Félix Leseur danced and talked a lot'.

On behalf of their son, his parents asked the Arrighis for their daughter's hand, and on Thursday 23 May 1889, they were officially engaged.

The marriage took place in their parish church of Saint-Germain-des-Prés, 31 July 1889. Sadly, Félix's father was unable to be there because of illness. One of Félix's former schoolmasters officiated, the Oratorian Fr Bordes, for whom he had a great respect; he called him a perfect religious and one who had had a great influence on him. According to French law, they then had a civil marriage at the Place Saint-Sulpice. They left in the afternoon for Fontainebleu and their new life together, but before they set off Elisabeth gave to Mamie a letter for her parents, thanking them for all that they had done for her:

> My dear parents, my heart is very full this moment; full of memories of my childhood and my youth which have returned with incredible force; full of confidence in the future for which you prepared me and that God will bless, I hope; but above all full of tenderness for you, for you all, more ardent, more profound than I have ever experienced before. Also, I feel the need to explain to you better perhaps than I have done before, that I want to thank you from the bottom of my heart for all the good you have done for me, for the happiness you have given me and which made my youth a time of such joy and a blessed memory; thank you for the tenderness with which you surrounded me; thank you for everything, for all that I have and for all that I am, it is from you I have received it.[1]

She assured them that her marriage would not change her feelings towards them, and that in Félix she had found everything she could wish for in a husband.

Their time in Fontainebleu passed far too quickly, in a happy dream, before they returned to Paris. The apartment they would have at 46 de la rue de l'Université was not yet ready for them, because it was a rather cold and uninviting apartment; Félix, who was fond of the good things of life, wanted it to be warm and comfortable, so they stayed in Elisabeth's old home while her parents and the other children were staying in Champrosay.

Their stay in Paris was very short because they were soon off on their travels, a continuation of their honeymoon. After visiting the Paris Exposition, they went to Luxembourg, sailed along the borders of the Rhine, visiting Trèves, Cologne and Spa. Writing to her uncle Alexandre, Elisabeth said, 'All this ravished me; all the time we were in such a delight and unimaginable silliness, and if there were two people on earth most happy, it was us'.

On their return they joined the family at Champrosey for a week; Félix then had to return to Rheims for a month, on 27 August, because he was called up to military service and attached to the 132nd Regiment as a reserve auxiliary doctor there.

After their whirlwind honeymoon, Elisabeth had time to reflect on their relationship, which had thrown up some disturbing revelations only a short while before their wedding. Although they had had a nuptial Mass, Félix had confided to her previously that he no longer believed in his Catholic Faith. It must have come as a shock to her, because, surrounded as he was by aunts, uncles, cousins, all with a strong faith, and being educated by the Oratorians whom he loved and much admired, who had given him a good religious education, she would have assumed that his faith was as strong as hers.

However, as Félix himself described, during his medical studies, he had begun reading the works of Montaigne and Rabelais, the main romantic writers, and others, of the 18th and 19th Centuries. He admitted that he had a somewhat frivolous side to his nature, a romantic bent and the usual tendency of youth to contradict those of the older generation, as well as a tendency to lecture others from his assurance of being in the right. 'All these things bubbled up in my brain,' he wrote, 'and contributed to rendering in me a very superficial and religious sentimentality.'[2]

When he began studying medicine in Rheims, before transferring to Paris, which was very much a centre of freethinking, this tenuous grasp on his faith was fatally undermined by the materialistic milieu of the university and the rigour of his medical studies. 'The medical teaching, around 1880, was entirely materialistic; its theories, like those of Broca on the cerebral locations, was accepted by everyone as if they were dogma', Félix wrote.

While he was at home, in order not to upset his parents, he continued his religious practices, but every time he returned to Paris his faith was being eaten away little by little, until to all intents and purposes he had passed very quickly into a practical paganism and atheism.

He had explained this to Elisabeth, and although it distressed her greatly, she had consented to the marriage going ahead, on the condition that he would allow her to continue to practice her faith.

Once Félix had completed his military duties, they went to stay with his parents; his brother Paul and his family were staying nearby in his in-law's country house, near Rheims, where their second son was born. The young couple came often to dine with Félix's parents, and they enjoyed the kindly family atmosphere there, which was all the more precious for suddenly being cut short.

For some while Elisabeth had felt very fatigued throughout September, and then, when Félix returned from his military service, she became confined to bed. The Leseur's family doctor diagnosed an abdominal abscess which had opened up in her intestine. There was grave concern that it could develop into peritonitis, with fatal consequences. Elisabeth was surrounded by the loving concern of the Leseur family, for whom she had become a second daughter, after the tragic death of their own daughter, Claire, at the age of only 22, the previous year. Also a welcome visitor was Auguste, who would stay with them on occasion during his many travels arranging exhibitions. He hated gloom and was a ray of sunshine for Elisabeth with his gaiety and laughter, during the tedium of her convalescence.

There was an excellent school of medicine in Rheims, so with her own husband a doctor, and with such good medical care of the time, Elisabeth managed to pull through, although she was never completely cured.

It was not until November that it was felt Elisabeth could make the journey back to Paris. She was put on a stretcher for the journey home, to their own apartment now ready for them on the rue de l'Université, where she immediately went to bed again for several more months. It was good for her to be back with her own family again, but that joy was to be short-lived. In December, her father was struck down by a virulent influenza that was sweeping the country, and within two days he had died. It was a devastating blow to the family, who loved him so much.

Elisabeth herself was too ill to attend the funeral, but the route of the cortège from the church to the cemetery was diverted to pass by her house. Elisabeth was laid on a chaise-longue by the window from where she could see the funeral procession. Their uncle Alexandre, who had never married, sold his apartment and went to live with the family, giving them, especially their mother, who had lost both a daughter and now her husband, the male support they needed.

Back in Paris, Elisabeth was given all the medical attention she required. Her doctors debated whether to carry out an operation, but it was deemed too dangerous. As Félix wrote later, 'Elisabeth was definitively condemned to look after her health for the rest of her life, and we had to arrange things accordingly'.[3] There was another sad loss when Félix's father died 22 April the following year at the age of 63.

By the summer, it was felt that Elisabeth's health had improved enough for them to move her to a place in the countryside in Marly-le-Roi, renting a small but beautiful house on the road to Saint-Germain. With her love for the countryside it would be more restful for Elisabeth than Paris. It also had the advantage of being near to some great friends of Félix, Maurice and Aimée Hennequin. Maurice was a well-known playwright, whose wife was Belgian, which made a special link with Félix, whose family had Belgian roots. Elisabeth was at once charmed by Aimée, who had a richly-endowed mind and vivacity, and who had for Elisabeth a real sympathy and a deep affection for her that never changed. The intellectual and artistic milieu that developed among the four of them was as much of a tonic to Elisabeth as the beautiful countryside. Neither Maurice nor Aimée were practicing Catholics, but they respected Elisabeth's beliefs, while she admired in Aimée her preoccupation with high ideals, good faith, integrity and honesty, which were so much in accord with Elisabeth's own character. Such was the rapport between them that from then on they went to stay with them every year.

The following year they joined the Hennequins in a chalet they rented at la Baule, together with Aimée's mother, brother and sister. They made trips out from there to Saint-Anne-d'Auray and le Morbihan. By then Elisabeth was recovered enough to accompany Félix to the annual congress in Rochefort of the Geographical Societies of France. Even while he was a student, Félix had been writing articles for magazines and journals on colonial affairs, which from the age of eleven and twelve had increasingly fascinated him. Geography had an irresistible attraction for him, and he was very much drawn towards studying colonial questions. The period from 1880 to 1900 was a time of great French political overseas expansion and exploration, in Africa and Asia in particular, and in Félix it grew from a boyish attraction to a settled intent to involve himself in some way in the colonies. He had decided that the best way was to study medicine, as this would be of great value to any overseas mission; he had no intention of practicing medicine in France itself. He became such an authority on colonial questions that he became more and more in demand for his expert knowledge.

After the congress, Elisabeth and Félix continued their journey through Royan, Bordeaux and Arcachon, returning by boat to Bordeaux and Saint-Nazare.

With their popularity, the Leseur household soon became a magnet, like those of their parents, for all that was best in Parisian society. The couple led a lively social life. They loved dining out and going to the theatre, especially the opera. Félix always enjoyed fine dining. Their friendship with the Hennequines opened doors to meeting people from all walks of the artistic life, the theatre, the music halls, the arts and literature.

1892 brought new joy to the Leseurs with first the marriage of Amélie to Maurice Duron, a doctor, in April. Then in December her brother Pierre married. The year also brought a change to Félix's interests. His articles on colonial questions had brought him into contact with Maurice Ordinaire, who was director of the militantly anticlerical journal '*Républic Française*'. The journal had been founded by Léon Gambetta, a Freemason and leader of moderate Republicans and, at the beginning of March Félix was invited to succeed Ordinaire as director. He accepted, but the following year moved to '*Siecle*', an equally anticlerical and anti-Catholic journal, so that he could write more extensively on colonial matters. These two were the most anticlerical journals in France and had a marked effect on Félix. Until then, he had tolerated Elisabeth's faith, sometimes going with her to Mass, but nothing more. Now he was mixing with politicians and journalists who had a real hatred of anything religious, especially of anything Catholic.

Félix began to stock his library with all the writers who were most opposed to the Church, and modernist writers such as Strauss, Renan, Sabatier and Loisy. He was, he said, looking for reasons to bolster his unbelief in the way that believers sought reasons for their belief. He became increasingly impatient and intolerant of anything that contradicted his atheism. He also became increasingly convinced that neutrality in the conflict between religion and atheism was impossible. 'It is possible, if need be, sometimes but very rarely, to be tolerant, the more often to be thought tolerant and to give the illusion of it, but to be neutral—never!'[4] Félix went on to quote Our Lord's own words that one had to be for him or against him, and for an atheist there was no other way than to oppose Jesus Christ and to oppose religion.

Félix aligned himself on the side of those against religion and made Elisabeth herself the object of his proselytising. Besides the library stocked with his books, the many visitors to their house were those he was meeting as part of his work as editor. It also gave him entry into the political sphere, and at that time France was becoming increasingly anti-Catholic.

His life was becoming more and more hectic, partly due to his own vivacious character and partly due to the artificial nature of the world of journalism where unforeseen events could quickly arise. He was often obliged to return late at night to the office to deal with last minute dispatches, where at times Elisabeth would join him; sometimes he did not get to bed until two or three o'clock in the morning. Otherwise, Elisabeth would use her time in the evenings, while Félix was out, in reading and studying.

Félix noted with satisfaction that from 1891, little by little, Elisabeth had been losing her practice of prayer and recollection which had been so much a part of her from childhood. She used her spare time in broadening her cultural and intellectual life. She had an enquiring mind that loved to seek out new horizons; Félix encouraged her in this, especially when, in 1892, she expressed a desire to learn Latin. The language suited her precise and logical mind and opened up to her all the treasures of the ancient world. Félix considered that the more he could direct her away from Christianity and towards humanism the better.

Elisabeth had a gift for languages; besides the English she learnt at school, she also became fluent in Russian and later began to study Spanish and Italian. As part of his growing atheism, between 1885 and 1900 Félix became enthralled by Russian literature such as Tolstoy, Dostoevsky and Turgenev. Elisabeth shared in his fascination and decided she wanted to read them in their original language. They also wanted to visit Russia when circumstances permitted, so to have some knowledge of the language would be helpful. Elisabeth began having lessons with a Russian high society lady who had retired to Paris and within two years she was fluent in speaking and writing it. When, in 1896, the Tsar and Tsarina visited Paris, Elisabeth took part in the celebrations. To mark the laying of the stone for the new Alexandre Bridge, it was decided that a group of young girls would come down the Seine in a flower-bedecked boat and present an exquisitely chased silver vase to the Empress. To Elisabeth's quiet amusement, no-one in the Government could speak Russian so, through the offices of their friend Ordinaire, Elisabeth was asked to give the address.

In May of 1893 Elisabeth and Félix visited Italy for the first time. Pupils from the Dominican College in Auteuil were going on a pilgrimage to Rome, and Mme Leseur was invited to go with them. She in her turn offered to pay for Elisabeth and Félix to join them. They visited the major cities of Italy, Naples, Florence, Venice, Genoa, Siena, Verona and Milan. In Rome, the pilgrims had an audience with the Pope, Leo X111. Félix found himself torn by many contradictions; seeing the Pope made a great impression on him, and in their tours he found himself surrounded on every side by Italy's Christian heritage, while at the same time he was adamant in his atheism.

For Elisabeth, the journey had special meaning, because it brought her closer to her Corsican background, when the Arrighis had settled in Genoa in the fifteenth Century, and she felt drawn to those ancient roots. Being surrounded also by her Christian past revitalised her faith, and the audience with the Pope made an indelible impression on her also.

There was more joy on their return, with the birth of her first niece, Marie, born to her sister Amélie 28 June, and her first nephew, Roger, her brother Pierre's first son, in October. More nephews and nieces were still to come, and for them all Elisabeth had a deep love. To her intense sorrow, because of her medical condition she herself was unable to have children; this was one of the greatest deprivations of her life, so she lavished on them all the resources of her rich maternal love.

Félix had never given up his desire for a position in the colonies, and he was helped in this by a friend of his, Delcassé, who had become Minister for the Colonies and offered Félix a post in the African Colonies. However, Elisabeth's family were deeply concerned at the effect that living in Africa would have on her precarious health. They did not have the same ambition as Félix and would not countenance seeing them leaving for the Sudan or Tonkin, and to Félix's credit, this opposition changed his plans.

Instead, the family offered him a position in their prestigious insurance company, the 'Conservateur' of which Elisabeth's uncle, M Picard, was director. Félix therefore took up his new post and relinquished all his colonial dreams, and on 1 January the following year, succeeded M Picard as director. It is a measure of the deep love and concern he had for Elisabeth and her health that he was willing to take such a momentous step and abandon his dreams.

That year increased the danger to Elisabeth's health and their friend Ordinaire invited them to spend some days with him in Jougne, in the high Jura, close to the Swiss border. The splendour of the countryside conquered the Leseurs totally and they began to think of having a house built there for themselves also.

They returned to Paris in August and one Sunday went with Félix's mother, his brother and his family for a trip to Pierrefonds. On their return through the forest the coachman manoeuvred the coach awkwardly, which overturned, and the horse caught Elisabeth under his hooves, kicking her several times in her side. They quickly got her back to their apartment, where she bled from a punctured liver, which again put her life in danger. She was bedridden for two months, but on her recovery the Leseurs took up their busy lifestyle again.

Despite Félix being forced to abandon his plans and being deprived of a post in the colonies, they both loved to travel, and not being posted abroad did not mean that they could not visit these remote and exotic places. The following year they were involved in a proposal to build a mosque in Paris, such as already existed in London, Manchester and in other big cities in Europe. Because of his colonial interest it was suggested that Félix could visit Algeria and Tunisia to gain the support of the Muslim people there for the undertaking, as well as obtain the financial support of the local rulers.

Félix saw from the joy in Elisabeth's eyes that she fully supported her husband and the thought of visiting these countries, and in April they set off on their travels.

Elisabeth kept a diary, in which she recorded her impressions and the people they met. This included Fr Delattre, a White Father who was an eminent expert in Punic, Roman and Christian antiquities. The White Fathers was a fairly newly-established missionary organisation founded by the Archbishop of Algiers, Cardinal Lavigerie in 1868. As well as their missionary work, the Fathers were influential in preserving the languages and culture of the indigenous peoples they served. Alfred Louis Delattre was perhaps the greatest White Father scientist at that time and easily bore comparison with the best archaeologists in his field. He spent his life digging the hill Byrsa in Carthage, Tunisia, in order to excavate the Punic, Roman and Christian remains there. His bibliography lists 250 publications and 25 other writings of importance.

While in Carthage, the Leseurs visited the museum he had set up to display the treasures he had unearthed. Elisabeth reflected on that great city, writing, 'Of all the different races that have lived within those walls, of all the wealth, the battles fought over it, there remains barely a trace'. It was a lesson in the impermanence of earthly kingdoms. They visited the little chapel dedicated to St Louis, and the site of the amphitheatre in which Saints Perpetua and Felicity had died. She revelled in the stunning scenery and brilliant flowers, the red poppies, yellow daisies and broom which scented the air and, as they reached the top of the hill, they saw Tunis spread out below them like a brilliant white cloth. In Marsa they were guests of the Bey, the ruler of Tunis, and took coffee with him.

Elisabeth returned home with her spirit and body refreshed, invigorated by this contact with a completely different culture and her mind expanded by what she had seen. The following year they therefore made the grand tour of Europe, visiting Munich, Bayreuth, Nuremberg,

Bamberg, Berlin, Dresden, Prague, Vienna, Budapest, Bucarest, the Carpathian mountains and the centre of Moldovia, returning by way of the Siniai, Budapest, Vienna, Salzburg and Innsbruck.

Their stay in Bayreuth in July was at the invitation of the composers who were close friends of theirs, Paul Hillemacher and Georges Hüe, where there were performances of Wagner's *Parsifal* and *Tetralogy*. Elisabeth recorded her impressions of *Parsifal*, which they both, with their love of Wagner, enjoyed immensely and which made a deep impression on her:

> In this admirable work, the religious sentiment was explained in a way I had never experienced before in any other work, so grand was it, in which one breathed in a divine perfume of forgiveness, love and purity which brought peace and which all the time imbued it.[5]

Félix was also highly satisfied, because both in her impressions of their tour of Tunis and in her impressions of *Parsifal* he noted that all her comments on the religious side of what they experienced did not awaken any spiritual response in her; she viewed everything, as he did, from the outside. Their worldly and busy lifestyle in Paris was also having its effect. He felt that his unceasing pressure on her to abandon her faith was now complete, and he could rest content.

Notes

[1] R. P. M-A. Leseur (Félix Leseur), *Vie d'Elisabeth Leseur* (Paris: J. de Gigord, Editeur, 1946), pp. 93ff.
[2] *Ibid.*, p. 105.
[3] *Ibid.*, p. 99.
[4] *Ibid.*, p. 108.
[5] *Ibid.*, p. 123.

3

CONVERSION

IN THE MIDDLE of 1898 Elisabeth said to Félix that she had nothing to read, and could he suggest something. Félix gave her a copy of *The Origins of Christianity* as well as the *Life of Jesus*, both by Renan, which he had in his library, saying they were very interesting and well written. He was confident that these books would be the final nail in the coffin of destroying Elisabeth's faith. With her exceptional and balanced intellect, her sure judgement, her excellent good sense, her strong culture, Félix felt sure she would be completely won over by Renan's arguments. Instead, exactly the opposite happened. Those very qualities enabled her to see through Renan's essential weakness; as she assessed it, the shallowness and poverty of his reasoning, his often contradictory and artificial assertions, his lack of sincerity at every turn. She wanted to go back to the source, to the Gospels in the first instance, to counter his arguments, and as she did so all of Félix's carefully constructed work of the previous years crumbled into dust. She was later to write:

> I read the Gospel, and by that sweet light I discover in myself many a nook of egotism and vanity. Unique book, perpetually read and perpetually new, supremely beautiful, resplendent with truth, of exquisite grace and charm, from which one can draw unendingly and never exhaust it![1]

Much later, Elisabeth looked back on that moment of her conversion:

> When I look back at the past, I see all my childhood and youth, even the beginnings of maturity, passed in ignorance of and estrangement from God. I see the first graces received while I was still young, although they did not sink in deeply; flashes from on high streaking across a path of indifference and superficiality; this call, a fugitive light glimpsed in the years of youth and swiftly extinguished, perhaps by a mysterious divine Will; the breaking of every link, even the external ones, with God and the total forgetfulness of Him in my heart; then the slow, silent action of Providence in me and for me; the wonderful work of conversion, begun, guided, completed by God alone, outside all human influence or contact, sometimes by the very means that should have caused me to lose all my religious faith, an action whose intelligent and loving beauty one could discern only when it was completed.[2]

With her new-found faith came the need for a new life-style, in which she had to carve out time for prayer, reflection and reading. As a child and with her methodical mind, she had drawn up a daily timetable for herself, although then more in the hope than in the execution. She now did the same thing, so that her time would be used to the best advantage but always bearing in mind the flexibility her status in life demanded.

She had found from bitter experience that the faith of her childhood and youth was insufficient to withstand the onslaught of atheism. She had now to develop it into the faith of an adult. Félix had amassed a library of atheistic and anti-Catholic literature; Elisabeth now built up a library of Catholic writers from the rich store that the Church possessed. Her favourite author was St Francis de Sales because his writings were addressed mainly to those living in the world, not to those in the cloister. She had the rare distinction of having an almost complete collection of his extensive writings. Much of Catholic spirituality came from the cloister to be adapted for lay people, but Elisabeth formed for herself a truly lay spirituality that would draw on the best of mystical tradition such as that of St Teresa of Avila and St Catherine of Siena, who, although nuns, were very much involved in the society in which they had lived. She built up a library of works of the early Church Fathers; she had the complete works of St Thomas Aquinas, as well as contemporary theologians. It was a well-balanced—and daunting—collection.

One difficulty for her in these first years of her conversion was that she was not able to find a priest who could guide her in her new life. By now they had moved from their apartment in the rue de l'Universitie to the rue d'Argenson and a new parish. She made her confession after her conversion in her new parish church of Saint-Augustin, without feeling that her parish priest was able to fill the role of spiritual director.

When Félix realised that his plan had failed, he was furious, especially since he had thought that victory had been assured. He therefore redoubled his criticism, his scorn, his assaults on the Catholic faith and Church. Before, with them both acknowledging their tendency to have a 'spirit of contradiction', with Félix in the full flush of his excitement and the conviction of his atheism, and with Elisabeth still under the influence of her childhood experiences of faith, they would undoubtedly have had some spirited but good-natured exchanges. Now, Félix's attacks had a very different and bitter tone, with him trying at every turn to belittle and besmirch his wife's newfound faith.

This gave an added dimension to Elisabeth's Catholic life; she had to tread a path of living with someone she loved deeply, who not only failed to understand what was now most precious to her but who was actively and resolutely opposed to it. It made in her spirit a deep well of loneliness and isolation that could have been soul-sapping, but she had to make something positive of it. A year after her conversion she decided to keep a diary where she could write about all the things she could not express openly in any other way. She opened her diary 11 September 1899:

> For a year I have been thinking and praying a great deal; I have tried unceasingly to enlighten myself, and in this perpetual labour my mind has matured, my convictions have become more profound, and my love of souls has increased, too. What is there greater than the human soul, or finer than conviction?
>
> We must create in ourselves a "new spirit," the spirit of intelligence and strength; we must renew ourselves and live our interior life with intensity. We must pray and act. Every day of our life must carry us nearer to the supreme Good and Intelligence—that is, nearer to God.[3]

This is an important entry, because it lays out in embryo the pattern of Elisabeth's whole life from now on. She was amassing her library of spirituality, but it was not a spirituality that remained in the study. Being genuine, it issued quite naturally into concern for others. As a child, she had mentioned in her diary that she had won a little bit of money at a game they were playing and noted that she had put it aside to give to the poor. This concern for the poor was fundamental to Elisabeth's journey into ever deeper union with God. It would never be a vague love of humanity as a whole but a totally individual thing, one person at a time, whatever their condition, religion or belief; indeed, she gave that love especially to those who were most different from her, as she wrote only a few days later:

> I want to love with a special love those whose birth or religion or ideas separate them from me; it is those especially whom I must try to understand and who need me to give them a little of what God has placed within me.[4]

This was not proselytising; it was first and above all trying to understand another's point of view without in any way compromising one's own grace: 'what God has placed within me'. It was from this way of understanding individual people, what motivated them and what was most dear to them, that she was able to broaden her horizon to a universal but never vague love.

Félix noted that from her conversion Elisabeth's 'spirit of contradiction' disappeared completely. She had learnt that 'It is not in arguing and lecturing that I can make them know what God is to the human soul', but, 'by struggling with myself, in becoming, with His help, more Christian and more valiant, I will bear witness to Him whose humble disciple I am. By the serenity that I mean to acquire I will prove that the Christian life is great and beautiful and full of joy'.[5]

In July of the year following her conversion, the Leseurs fulfilled their desire to visit Russia, and for which Elisabeth had learnt Russian. They also took in Finland and Poland. Elisabeth found that her Russian came in very useful and was delighted that she was easily able to make herself understood. She began, in the train taking them there, speaking in Russian to one of the attendants on the train. She wrote on a postcard she sent to her mother 'I'm understood, and I can understand, and that amused me greatly'.

They enjoyed the magnificent scenery they saw; they marvelled at the Hermitage museum; they visited the Winter Palace and the Smolensk monastery, but they were bitterly disappointed in the experience of being in Russia itself. There was the constant police surveillance; they felt themselves surrounded by people who had nothing in common with them, with closed minds, under a political and social state that had been held back for many years.

The Leseurs were so disillusioned with the whole situation in Russia that they changed their travel plans and left for Constantinople with a sense of relief and freedom after the oppressive atmosphere they had left behind. They went through Turkey, Greece and Italy before returning home to Paris, and to an exhausting round of activity. Elisabeth began 1900, the start of a new century, by pondering on the Communion of Saints, a doctrine that would have an increasing and deepening meaning for her:

> I believe that no humble unknown act or thought, seen by God alone, is lost, and that all, in fact, serve souls. I believe, according to a saying I love, that 'when we do good we know not how much good we do'.[6]

Therefore she had to work continually on herself to accomplish that inner transformation, by increasing in a love which would continually remake her into the image of Christ, not simply for her own salvation, but even more because 'Such love could save the world'.

> Why groan, when with such a love one might act?
> Why hate, since hate destroys, when that divine love can bring life and transformation to hearts? [7]

After visiting the Paris Exposition they travelled to Spain in April, returning after five weeks, in May, via Tunis, which they preferred to Spain. By contrast with other journeys which she had enjoyed only on the material level, during these journeys she was continuing to reflect on her life, which she felt had before been so often empty and useless. With God in her life now, although everything about her life remained outwardly the same, she was more and more convinced that the least thing she did in her life could be of value in transforming herself, to the benefit of souls.

In July they travelled to Germany and Luxembourg, staying with their good friends the Hennequins by the banks of the Meuse. Elisabeth had a deep love for her country, and they arrived at Metz on their journey home, which, she said, made a painful impression on her. It was 'French in appearance and population, German in its innumerable soldiers and barracks.' It was a part of Lorraine now under German occupation, which pained her deeply, but immediately her thoughts turned to something far nobler than winning it back by force of arms. The French were still a great people, she wrote in her diary, but by making 'the name of *Frenchman* synonymous with justice, light and moral force':

> We must become a people truly strong, not only by force of arms—that is too little—but by the valiant nobility of character of all of us, from the humblest to the greatest. Chastity, determination, and the dignity of life should be perpetually taught and developed in all. Woman, whose immense role and influence the French do not yet fully grasp, and who does not always grasp it herself, should from now on realise her task and consecrate her life to it.[8]

Elisabeth did not need to point out that this transformation had to begin with herself above all, and only then could it radiate out to others. She was also increasingly convinced about the vital, indispensible role that women had in the renewal of her country, as in any country. Another aspect of her love for France was that, far from this love narrowing her outlook towards other peoples, it made her appreciative of how others felt about their own countries, histories and traditions.

The rest of that summer was spent going back and forth between Paris and the country, entertaining various acquaintances and being entertained. In September they were back in Paris where Elisabeth could enjoy the calm and study her Latin authors, reading Horace and Juvenal in the original; she found it fascinating to enter into a society so different from her own. This was not just head knowledge; it informed her way of looking at the lifestyles and beliefs of others around her, and, in her own social milieu, to be open to what they could tell her. Recording discussions with friends who were unbelievers she noted that there were those 'whom divine light does not illuminate, or rather whom it illuminates in a manner unknown to us with our restricted minds.'[9]. This lies at the root of her extreme delicacy in approaching others, and the respect she had for those who did not believe as she did. There was the understanding that God could be working in them, in his own time and in his own way, and she had to be responsive whenever she felt that God could use her to help them come more into his light.

She was also reflecting on social questions and was convinced that only through Christianity could society develop in material, intellectual and moral ways. This was because she believed only Christianity was concerned with the place of each person and their place in the world and in society, as an individual, in what was most intimate in him and what was able to renew him from within. Foremost and above all, each person was a son or daughter of God, made in his own image and likeness, uniquely loved by him, and created for an eternal destiny.

She was, as always, reading the New Testament and:

> The further I read into the Gospels and Epistles, the more do I find a charm, a strength, a life that is incomparable. God is indeed there; from this reading

> I come each day calmed and strengthened; my will is reinforced there and my heart warmed. God, the Supreme Teacher, through this book of books, educates my inmost being. It helps me to understand life, to smile at duty, and to will strongly.[10]

She needed that calm and strength the following year, when her nephew, Roger, who was the son of Félix's brother, Paul, became seriously ill. Her mother and Juliette had left for Italy in April; Paul's younger son Pierre, made his First Communion 9 May. The day after, Roger became violently feverish. Her mother and Juliette arrived back 12 May and the following day, at eight o'clock in the evening, he died; he was only nine years old. The whole family was devastated. Elisabeth, with her strong conviction of eternity, wrote later, 'He left us quietly for eternity, and the veil between the two worlds seemed light indeed',[11] but with her deep love for all her nephews and nieces also felt devastated by the loss.

After the sadness of Roger's death Félix and Elisabeth stayed in Savoy for two weeks at the end of July and then went on to Holland. Elisabeth found the landscape rather melancholy, preferring countries of light such as Greece, Italy and the East, countries of 'those beautiful, gentle colours, where all looks so harmonious'. Halfway through their stay she began to feel very tired; she insisted that they continue their tour, but suddenly she became ill with a flare-up of the hepatitis that had mostly remained dormant since her childhood. Félix did not want her being ill in an unfamiliar country, so they returned quickly to France. Her mother was staying with the Durons, and as M Duron had also become Elisabeth's doctor, they stayed with them at Marly. Surrounded by her family, she made a good recovery, writing in October:

> Days of great interior happiness, rich in firm resolutions. I am going to fill my life with work and charity and the accomplishment of duty, all my duty.[12]

With the New Year, though, her ill health returned:

> Bodily fatigue, domestic troubles, and worse than that, a kind of sadness and moral apathy, a lack of the fervour and inner joy that God has sometimes given me so abundantly. And yet not for a moment has my will ceased to belong to Him; duty has cost me dearly, but it has not ceased to be duty.[13]

There was great joy for her later that year when the whole family went to share the summer together at Jougne. Since the Hennequins had first invited them to stay with them there, it had become a very special place for them both, and by 1902 they had fulfilled their dream of having a villa of their own built there. It was the family home she had always wanted for herself, and since it was a home for all her extended family she delighted in the sounds of her nephews and nieces laughing and playing, the joy of friends who would stay with them, the company of their parents, brothers and sisters. It would remain a much-loved family home for them all, even after Elisabeth's death, passing on to her niece Marie.

It also gave her the space and tranquillity she craved—the children knew not to disturb her first thing in the morning which was her time for quiet prayer. Her spirit expanded in the calm and magnificent surroundings. She loved the village church which she would visit each day and where she could attend Mass. She became involved in the life of the parish and the village during their stays there.

Writing in July to a close family friend, the painter Charles-Jules Duvent, she described a little of their life there:

> The first days passed here have been so full that I haven't had the time to write, and so I wanted to

tell you that I'm thinking of you in this beautiful countryside. There is absolute calm, and I'm writing to you in front of our beautiful valley, our forest of fir trees, of all the marvellous view that we have from the terrace of the house ... I have become a gardener, pulling up weeds, removing stones, and looking to and giving our garden a less arid aspect than it has ... That which is giving me deep joy is to have around me all our families and above all the children, so that I can work and talk and play with them and pass delightful times.[14]

This first time in their new home was interrupted when Félix received an urgent summons to go to Austria on his company's business, and since they were never separated Elisabeth went with him, despite the sadness she felt at leaving her beloved Jougne. She took Juliette with her and together they explored Vienna, which she had visited briefly in 1897. It was a sad return to Jougne, though, because while they were away her mother's cousin, who was staying there with them, whom the whole family loved and treated as a grandparent, had a sudden heart attack as he went up to his room, and died.

The whole village rallied round them, taking his body to a reception room in the town hall where local people kept vigil with him throughout the night. As if that wasn't sadness enough, during the services a telegram arrived telling them that her brother's mother-in-law had been injured in a car accident. Her sister-in-law left immediately to look after her.

Writing to a close friend, Jeanne, she paid a fitting tribute to the local people who had been so good to them and whose character she appreciated:

> In seeing these people so sane, so dignified, and so united, I said to myself that those who sow hatred are very culpable. I know well that they are tainted

by 'superstition' and to the eyes of some everything is fine like that. But even for those, like me, who do not share these superstitions, one can still wonder if the beautiful and strong local and family customs, the respect of all who deserve respect, that narrow solidarity that binds them together and that manifests itself through some works and a very interesting organisation—if all these things that are obviously the fruit of superstition do not have a value that one hesitates to destroy. I would like to bring Georges here and notice with him these spirited people, very proud and free, who have nothing of the 'religious' in the bad sense of that word. There are two women religious here who render unappreciated services and who are probably going to leave like the others when the 'new order' begins.[15]

There is a lot to read between the lines in this letter. Her reflection on the 'superstitions' the local people mingled with their Catholic faith may have been caused by Félix's response to these practices. He would undoubtedly have rejected all of it, Catholic beliefs as well as the 'superstitions', not distinguishing between them, and this would have had the effect of confirming him in his contempt for all religion. Elisabeth's reaction was much more nuanced. In many Catholic countries, practices have persisted from their pagan past and which the Church has been unable to eradicate. The Church's practice has been to look for what is good in other religions and show how they are fulfilled in Christ. In the early days of the Church, for example, as she expanded and paganism declined, she often took over pagan temples and dedicated them as Christian churches. Elisabeth did not agree with the pre-Christian practices, but with her openness of mind, nurtured by their travels and her appreciation of beliefs that differed from her own, she could see beyond them to the excellent qualities of the local people, and also the way they were not '"religious" in the bad sense of the word'. By this she might have meant the natural way their religion was totally embedded in their lives, without pretence.

In the letter she also referred to the two religious, women who would have to leave, and this was due to the 'Law of Associations' which had recently been promulgated by the violently anti-Catholic and anti-religious Government. The Minister for the Interior, Pierre Waldeck-Rousseau, had, in 1901, passed the Associations Bill. This Bill brought all religious institutions under the control of the State, to ensure the supremacy of the civil power. He resigned 3 June 1902, considering that he had fulfilled his mission. He was succeeded by Emile Combes; who, like Waldeck-Rousseau, came from a Catholic background. He had even begun studying for the priesthood before rejecting the Catholic Faith completely. He later became a Freemason and a spiritualist.

On taking office he stated that his sole purpose was to destroy all the religious orders, and he set about the task with anti-clerical zeal. He refused *en masse* the applications of teaching and preaching congregations for official recognition under the Law of Associations and was particularly harsh on the teaching orders. He closed thousands of their schools, forcing the religious to flee the country; thousands of chapels were also closed or threatened with closure. Basically, the Catholic faith was permitted to exist only if it remained behind closed doors.

Writing to Charles Duvent, Elisabeth expressed her anger and concern at what was happening in Jougne itself:

> Listen to this: The superior general of the Sisters of Charity of Besançon when the vote was taken on the law of associations, went to find the prefect to ask him what she ought to do. He said to her

that given the Congregation had kept the previous laws they had nothing to fear and need do nothing. The superior went to Paris to find Waldeck-Rousseau, who used the same language. She returned with peace of mind and in ten days they will expel them. What do you say to that?[16]

She knew that she had in Charles, a practising Catholic, one who supported her in her concerns, but certainly she would not have found it in Félix, who was presumably enthusiastic in support of the Law. Elisabeth wondered whether the close union between the civil element and the religious element which she had found working at her uncle's funeral, but in such a diluted expression, would be able to withstand the force behind this new law.

It was not an easy return to Paris for her as she took up her duties, back to the empty busyness of life there, without her family and the children around her. It was not helped, either, by the news that a friend, Alice Sachs, was divorcing her husband, at a time when divorce was very rare and the first within her circle of friends. Alice, young and charming, wanted to live her life and to affirm her right to happiness which Elisabeth called 'the right to cause hurt to others'. Elisabeth had a deep affection for her, seeing in her qualities she did not in fact have, and when reality dawned on her, she could not blame her. She tried to dissuade Alice from the path she was taking, and when this proved fruitless, it damaged their friendship, something that hurt Elisabeth greatly. All this had sapped her energy, and when she returned home she put her thoughts down on paper as to how she would confront the problem:

> I feel that all my knowledge, assisted by that inner light and grace of which the trace is so apparent in my life, must be a knowledge of reconciliation. I must simply and strongly profess a faith that God

has gradually created in me. But I must do this in a way that never harms or offends the convictions or its absence in others. I must relinquish, unknown to anyone, my tastes and preferences, everything but the principles by which I live.[17]

Alice had broken up her home in order to remarry but it also caused a storm in the Leseur household. Alice was intending to marry a close friend of Félix, and of course Félix supported her in her decision. He flew into a rage at Elisabeth's opposition, the only real disagreement they had in the whole of their marriage, although she kept calm and tried to explain her reasons. Such calmness, when Félix was trying to persuade her to his own way of thinking, always had the effect of riling him even more! She felt that the milieu in which they moved, rich, dilettante, without any deep moral roots, but which was just the milieu that Félix enjoyed and Elisabeth now did not, was the cause of such a flippant attitude towards the institution of marriage, among other things. Fortunately, their own marriage and the deep love each had for the other, weathered this disagreement.

Notes

[1] E. Leseur, *My Spirit Rejoices* (Manchester, New Hampshire: Sophia Institute Press, 1996), p. 50.
[2] *Ibid.*, pp. 167ff.
[3] *Ibid.*, p. 45.
[4] *Ibid.*
[5] *Ibid.*, p. 51.
[6] *Ibid.*, p. 48.
[7] *Ibid.*, pp. 48ff.
[8] *Ibid.*, p. 52.
[9] *Ibid.*, pp. 54ff.
[10] *Ibid.*, p. 54.
[11] *Ibid.*, p. 59.

[12] *Ibid.*, p. 62.
[13] *Ibid.*, p. 65.
[14] R. P. M.-A. Leseur (Félix Leseur), *Vie d'Elisabeth Leseur* (Paris: J. de Gigord, Editeur, 1946), pp. 53ff.
[15] J. K. Ruffing RSM (edited, translated and introduced by), *Elisabeth Leseur* (New York: Classics of Western Spirituality, Paulist Press, 2005), p. 198.
[16] *Ibid.*, p. 299ff, note 6.
[17] *Ibid.*, p. 68.

4

CONFRONTING UNBELIEF

THE ATTACKS ON the Church were not the only issues that Elisabeth faced with revulsion. There was the ongoing 'Dreyfus Affair', which began in 1894, when compromising French military documents, apparently handed to the Germans, were found in a waste paper basket in the German Embassy. A scapegoat had to be found, and with no evidence whatsoever, a certain Captain Alfred Dreyfus was alleged to have been the culprit. He was a member of a wealthy textile-manufacturing family of Alsatian Jews; his race alone was considered enough to convict him and he was sent to the notorious Devil's Island. Over the years the debate raged as to whether he really was guilty or not, with such ferocity that it almost brought down the Republic. It inevitably gave rise to anti-semitism, and in her diary Elisabeth recounted a conversation she had had with friends of hers, the Alcans, who were non-practising Jews. It was doubly distressing to Elisabeth that it was fellow Catholics who were the most vehemently anti-Dreyfus. The Archbishop of Paris became patron of the Laborum League of anti-semitic army officers, and in its journal, *La Croix*, the Assumptionist Order inflamed the situation, which led in its turn to greater anti-clerical feeling. An even more damaging consequence of the Assumptionist's campaign was the 1902 Law of Associations, which was passed largely in response to it. It was against this background that Elisabeth wrote in her diary 28 November 1901:

> Talked to [Emile Alcan] and his wife yesterday about the unjust and unchristian treatment of Jews in

> certain circles. My God, will you not give to poor human beings a spirit of intelligence and wisdom, which is the gift of your eternal Spirit? Will you not awaken soon in them the spirit of charity that you came to bring into the world, and which you said contained 'the law and the prophets?'. I wish I could organise a holy crusade against hate and promote justice among men and women. At any rate, in this garden God has given me to cultivate, I want to plead by my attitude, my words, and my actions before everyone I meet the great cause of charity.[1]

She had started that crusade within herself already, and her influence would spread. She expressed herself even more forcefully in an entry in her 'Daily Thoughts':

> Fanaticism fills me with horror, and I cannot understand how it can exist with sincere conviction. Can anyone who loves Christianity passionately and wishes to see it reign in souls think for one moment that he should use any method to achieve this goal other than persuasion? Can one instil conviction through force or deceit? Besides, is there not in the use of such means something completely repugnant to the upright loyal spirit that should mark every sincere Christian? And yet how many little acts of fanaticism we commit unconsciously?[2]

Fanaticism of any sort hurt her deeply, but there is an intriguing possibility, that the anti-semitism she met with affected her more profoundly; because her uncle's name, Barthelemy-David, had Jewish connotations there might have been Jewish ancestry in her family.

While she was hurt deeply by fanaticism and lack of charity among Catholics, she was only too well aware of the fanaticism, the lack of charity, of understanding and respect in the atheists and the anti-clerical friends in her own circle, including, of course, her own husband. She had very early on, after her return to the Faith, realised that argument and discussion when the other side were unwilling to listen to contrary arguments, got nowhere. For her part, once she had realised the futility of arguing for her faith, she resolved that she would make every effort to listen with respect to views that were opposed to her own. Her friend Aimée Fiévet described her impressions of Elisabeth during these discussions:

> When she did not approve of a judgment, an idea expressed and she had reason to keep silent ... She neither protested by an expression on her face, nor by critique. From her silence emanated something inexpressible giving the impression that she had withdrawn into her soul, like putting something away in a safe place.
>
> She was a good listener, looking for the truth or wisdom of her interlocutor. Some discussions were very profound and prolonged ... At other times in intimate conversations, her face took on an extraordinary appearance, as if she wanted to understand completely what was being said ... and expressed it, especially if it was a matter of education, morality, or duty, etc. If they did not come to agreement, she would end ... easily, with a smile full of resolve and hope and say, 'we will think about this each from our own side'. Elisabeth was very clear-sighted and intuitive, often understanding something that had not been said. If she thought she might be helpful or useful, she would make the perfect response with discretion, without giving the impression of an intrusive intimacy.[3]

The Leseurs knew Aimée Fiévet when she was a young philosophy student, and she often came to their house. At this time she was enthused by the philosophy of Bergson, which was all the rage among students. One such evening Félix spoke somewhat mockingly and condescendingly about her enthusiasm and after she had left, Elisabeth spoke to her husband about his attitude. She herself considered Bergson to be a 'flawed mirror', but even so, he was opening up to these young people a little of the spiritual world in a way that they might not otherwise experience. As such, she could not bring herself to 'quench the flickering flame' and begged her husband not to do so himself.

Aimée later became *Directrice de l'Ecole Municipale Superieur Sophie German*, and so she and Elisabeth had a shared concern about female education. An unbeliever, she was also an inspector of schools and was keen to implement the atheist reforms brought in by the Government. While these reforms were removing any religious influence from schools, something which concerned Elisabeth deeply, they were also promoting education for girls, which she supported wholeheartedly.

Despite their opposing views about the place of religion in education, Elisabeth acknowledged that she and Aimée had many things in common, and this provided a strong base for their friendship: 'We do not have the same ideas about everything, I know, and my beliefs are not fully yours,' she wrote. Nevertheless, they shared a love of truth and concern for others; they both loved whatever was good, true and beautiful, and Elisabeth felt at ease with her enough to share her inner thoughts, and what mattered most to her, her faith. Aimée, for her part, had a high opinion of Elisabeth, saying, after Elisabeth's death, 'In spite of our very different lives, Elisabeth was one of my friends to whom my thoughts turned and still turn most often. Some beings are a light toward which all turn who need light to live by!'[4]

Confronting Unbelief

In parallel with her Diary, Elisabeth also jotted down her 'Resolutions', and in them, from the very beginning of her return to the Faith, was the sense that she was being called to a very particular vocation; since God had treated her like a 'privileged child', she felt he had prepared her for an intellectual apostolate. She had been well prepared for this, with her active, enquiring mind, her social standing which enabled her to mingle and speak with the greatest minds in France: artists, politicians, writers, scientists. She had travelled widely, with an open mind and heart, meeting people of different cultures and beliefs. She read widely on social issues, from Latin writers of the pre-Christian era, the Church Fathers, the two-thousand-year repository of Christian thought and belief, Russian literature and issues concerning the France of her day. It was from this rich background that she felt she had an apostolate to reach out in Christian love to whoever needed her, whether in simple friendship or with sharing her beliefs.

She recognised that she had the ability to discern this 'intimate and personal action in the depths of the human soul', and so:

> In obliging me to live in the midst of total negation and indifference and that impenetrable ignorance of divine things that oppresses so many unfortunate people, He has doubtless intended that I should have compassion for, share myself with, and turn toward those who blaspheme and doubt with more pity and love.[5]

This meant that she had to cultivate her own mind, 'methodically to increase knowledge of all those subjects that my mind is ready to seize upon and study,' and to do it from a spiritual motive. It meant great discernment, knowing when to speak if she felt it would help someone and would be received, and when to keep silent, if a response would only arouse more antagonism.

She would never compromise her own principles, simply allowing the other person to have the freedom to disagree, but to speak of her own faith simply and clearly if she felt it was right to do so. She made an interesting observation that she was:

> struck with the fact that unbelievers have more sympathy with people of deep faith than with those of variable and utilitarian views. These dear unbelievers attend more to those who are 'intransigent' regarding the Faith than to those who by subtlety and compromise hope to bring them to accept the Faith. And yet the bold statement must be made with the most intelligent sympathy and the liveliest and most delicate charity.[6]

She had to walk a fine line when taking in at a deep level what was being said, when she might not agree with it, while retaining her own beliefs, at the same time being open to the other person's belief and the good it might contain, which was so important to them:

> Not to accept everything, but to understand everything; not to approve of everything, but to forgive everything; not to adopt everything, but to search for the grain of truth that is contained in everything.[7]

It was difficult for her to have two conflicting approaches, one, to those with whom she could share her faith, in the way of friendship, and yet to conceal it to others, especially to the one closest to her, her husband.

With her friend Aimée they could share a love for nature, for all things good, true and beautiful, and for Elisabeth that would draw her soul inexorably to the God of all good, truth and beauty. For Aimée it was different.

She looked at the inexorable march of time, and saw no hand of God in it, as she wrote to Elisabeth:

> Seeing these waves that, for centuries, follow one another, crashing on the beach, and the huge patterns that erase themselves, I see that they move with the same indifference as the wreckage that floats on the surface, plants, animals, and people—in which all mixed together in destruction, life and death.[8]

Such a pessimistic outlook did affect her, and she did give way to feelings of isolation and depression, from which Elisabeth gently and compassionately tried to lift her. In reply, Aimée said that 'this supreme equality' calmed her by showing her the unity of everything around her, and that therefore she felt a solidarity with all things and a need to go out to others in love. She did not believe in the immortality of the soul, so this life was all she had in which to show love for others.

Their friendship was such that Aimée was able to express her misgivings when she attended the baptism of her grand-niece and the place in the ritual for cleansing the young child from original sin. This did not, of course, imply any personal sin in the child, but the tendency to sin in all mankind, which could surely be acknowledged, because 'time changes nothing because evil always exists here below'. This concept of sin was, as Elisabeth acknowledges, somewhat alien to the contemporary mind; Aimée denies it, but a Christian cannot, for without the concept—and the reality—of sin, baptism would be superfluous.

Elisabeth urges her friend to take a rounded look at Christianity, because everything in it fits together, and if one tried to dislodge one brick from the building the whole edifice would collapse. This is not to say that Christianity is built on shaky foundations, but that all is intimately intertwined and even the most seemingly trivial part of it is based on the great, basic and dominant truths of the Faith. Continuing the metaphor of a building, and using an illustration she had taken from elsewhere, Elisabeth compares it to the stained-glass windows in a church. 'When you see the exterior windows of a church, you see only some unformed fragments, but from inside, it is colourful and harmonious'.[9]

Replying to this letter, Aimée felt that she had annoyed or pained Elisabeth by this criticism, but Elisabeth refers playfully back to the discussion, responding, 'You really deserved to be scolded for having sinned in thought'. Rather than being upset, Elisabeth rejoices in the candour with which they can both express themselves to each other. However, she does take exception to Aimée saying that she felt Elisabeth had made her convictions and the Catholic faith fit to her own size, and that, as Aimée put it, 'elevated, purified and divinized' them. Along with many atheists, Aimée could only conceive that the Christian faith constricted its believers rather than offer them sublime goals to which they could aspire.

By no means, responds Elisabeth, the opposite is true. It is only the slow and transforming action of God within her that was drawing her ever closer to the light and giving her even just a glimpse of the glory and splendour of God's life. Aimée seemed to think, she said, that most Christians lived under vaulted ceilings concealing the sky, but that in her friend's case there were no longer 'walls constricting the air you breathe'.[10]

'In what way is my sky obscured, or where are the walls that limit my horizon?' Elisabeth asks. Yes, she accepts all the teachings of the Church, and its moral laws, but in what way does that differ from Aimée's own fight against self-centredness, hatred and evil in all its forms, as she does? They both accept scientific laws, and Aimée does not feel herself constrained by believing only in those things that can be verified by scientific means:

> I would reply that the truths in the spiritual order are verified by the soul, with the aid of other methods, without doubt, but which are also certain. And they are assimilated like our human organism assimilates nourishing bread. Religious truth is not a passive thing; it is alive and we sense its all-powerful reality when it has taken possession of our being, illuminated it, transformed it, strengthened it. To continue, and this is a certain point, the little that I value must be in my faith or it will not be me.[11]

With another friend, Jeanne Alcan, her atheist Jewish friend, she stresses her belief that practices in the Christian life can have their parallel in the secular life. In one letter, she suggests a method that her mother had recommended to her as a teenager. Jeanne was having difficulty in organising her life, so Elisabeth suggests that she:

> Do regularly each day that which you are supposed to do: your accounts, a little personal work, intellectual and physical ... I am convinced that these small, repeated actions will restore the vigour of your will, which is a little anaemic, and that you will feel the good effects.[12]

This is what Elisabeth herself practised in her own busy life, and she also recommends the secular version of her daily time set apart for prayer and meditation. She is not suggesting that she is forcing Jeanne into a Christian practice, 'but there are some thoughts that are common to all humanity, and some reflections on duty, on usefulness and the meaning of life, on love of one's fellow human beings, that everyone can do, it seems to me, whether believers or unbelievers'.[13]

In this way Elisabeth could translate aspects of her Catholic faith into a secular version, if that would help her friend. When Jeanne was finding it difficult to cope with her family life and its obligations Elisabeth drew on her own experience to help her. She, too, knew the difficulties of balancing her many social and charitable obligations with running her household, and with sharing in the concerns of her extended family and friends. She always tried to begin her day with a time for quiet prayer and meditation, to set the tone of her day, to take time to look at the things she had to do that day and put them in reasonable order. She recommends 'what in religious language is called a preview of the day'.

> That is, take a rapid look at all the tasks that will fill your day and make resolutions about how you want to do them. And in the evening, you might also make a short examination of conscience to make sure that you have given to others that which they can rightfully expect from you.[14]

At the end of the day she would make, in time-honoured Catholic tradition, an 'examination of conscience', a review of the day and how she had used it well. She advised Jeanne to do something similar in a secular context and also, or even especially, the practice of prayer. She introduced her to the doctrine so dear to her heart, the Communion of Saints, giving a brilliant and concise explanation of it and suggesting the secular version of it, which would be the equivalent of prayer:

> Christians believe that a mysterious, spiritual solidarity exists among themselves and all other children of the same God. We call this solidarity the communion of saints, the efforts, merits and sufferings of each individual benefit the rest. A similar law exists in the natural order, and if we

think about it a little, we shall be convinced that our words and actions have a deeper and more far-reaching effect than we often imagine.'[15]

From this it follows that everyone, believer or non-believer, should think carefully on what they say and do, knowing that it might affect others. 'There is no neutrality in matters of morality.' So 'let us create an interior treasure of noble thoughts, energy and strong, intense affection, and then we may be sure that sooner or later, perhaps without our being aware of it, the overflow will affect the hearts of others'.[16]

Elisabeth gained another sparring partner when her childhood friend, Yvonne Le Gros, wrote to her to say that she was engaged to, as Elisabeth delightfully dubbed him, her 'own Félix', Félix le Dantec. Like her own husband, Félix le Dantec was an atheist, a Professor of Theology at the Sourbonne and had written a couple of books on the subject. Elisabeth invited the couple to join them for lunch so that, as she put it, she would not 'be taken as a villain, let him see in advance that his future adoptive sister-in-law is not "a servant of obscurantism". Moreover, (at least, I hope), that I have not been made into a fanatic or a frightful reactionary'.[17]

Unsurprisingly, the conversation at the lunch turned to religion, and Elisabeth found him 'so ignorant, so savant, on religious matters, in this great shell of materialism with which he is encased, that it is impossible to pierce through'.

Le Dantec said that his religious upbringing conflicted with his scientific training, and Elisabeth tried to show him that the two were not incompatible. The discussion was very intense, and she felt that she had shaken his certainty a little, with le Dantec saying, at the end, that her arguments were stronger than that of the priest with which he had engaged in discussion in his book '*Le Conflit*'.

While she was recuperating at Jougne, 1907 Elisabeth read his books, *L'Atheisme* and *Les influences ancestral*, as well as *Le Conflit*, and decided to answer some of the objections to religious belief that he attacked in them, with her typical lightness of touch. She was not competent to discuss some of his scientific ideas, she said, but she could respond from the 'terrain of religion', to which she had definite inside knowledge, and to which he had some objections. She enjoyed not finding him to be a logical atheist 'because you would not be the charming person whom we love so fraternally':

> Is it not unusual and striking to think that finding for the first time in my life a true atheist, that I must establish the admirable qualities of this latter that are his due, not only an exceptionally rich nature, but even more these 'ancestral errors' that enliven many souls and upon which mine has nourished itself.[18]

Typically, Elisabeth recognises the goodness and integrity she saw in him, but she said that it created within her a sense of sadness. She felt that a true believer would not be swayed by his arguments, but they might persuade one who was already three quarters of the way towards atheism to go the whole way. The problem she had with his detached scientific approach was that the area of religious belief escapes the scientific domain:

> You want to convince us of our absurdity through arguments that do not convince us, because we will be able to respond that whereas you argue in order to persuade us that we are unreasonable, we 'live' from a higher life, entirely interior, so penetrated with faith that our moral being is transformed by it and that at the same time we are able to remain very

humble, since we feel that this life has been given to us and that we do not believe this on our own.[19]

It is the difficulty that many believers have when discussing matters of faith with unbelievers. Very often, the straw man that the atheist puts up is so far removed from the believer's faith and experience that it is irrelevant; then, the dialogue progresses on parallel lines, because the unbeliever has never experienced the certainty of being grounded in the truth that faith gives.

Elisabeth ends her letter to him by pardoning her 'small expression of "mysticism" ', as she describes her faith, and then concludes by saying, somewhat mischievously, that 'you are a bit of a mystic just as you are a bit Christian, just as you are especially one of the best hearts I have known'.[20] In response, Le Dantec's opinion of Elisabeth was that she was 'at the summit of humanity'.[21]

Félix became very much a part of the Leseur family circle, treated as almost a second brother. The date of their marriage had to be postponed due to Félix falling ill; he needed to leave Paris and rest for a while in cleaner air. Sadly, it was a portent of his early death from tuberculosis at the age of 48. Félix and Yvonne were finally married later that year 19 October 1905, in the church of Saint-Germain-de Près. In keeping with that nobility and openness of spirit that Elisabeth had discerned in him, unlike others of his atheist friends Félix was happy to entertain priests and Christian friends and to listen to their beliefs with respect, especially out of respect for Yvonne's faith. And so, although he was never reconciled to the Church, to the fury of his anti-clerical and atheist friends he was buried with Catholic funeral rites, because, he said, 'We can't take from those who believe the only means of reassurance and consolation which remains for them in a time of mourning; I feel that would be criminal'.

In introducing Jeanne to the belief in the Communion of Saints, and its secular equivalent in the human solidarity in which what one person does can have unknown consequences for unnumbered others, Elisabeth recognised that this is a difficult task for one who relied on reason alone, 'which to some extent is only a tool'. Nevertheless, she was convinced that God worked in every person, even though they might not know it or acknowledge it. An atheist would never address God personally, but they could 'yet offer genuine homage by their love of the good, the just, and the beautiful. I believe that God inspires and directs all true reason and all who walk by its light'.[22]

Therefore, she could set aside ways of talking about her faith and talk about the shared humanity they had as rational beings:

> I want to limit myself to the sphere that belongs to all, Christians and unbelievers alike. For Christians are also 'rational beings', and reason brings them just as far as anyone else, namely, up to the point of which Pascal speaks, 'reason's last step is the recognition that there is an infinite number of things which are beyond it'.[23]

To Elisabeth, this was a limitation. For herself, she had, not only her reason, which she cultivated assiduously into a fine instrument, but also her faith, which opened up literally infinite vistas for her beyond, but not against, reason.

Because it meant so much to her, she suffered interiorly when her faith was attacked, noting one such incident:

> Bitter suffering of an evening spent in hearing my faith and spiritual things mocked at, attacked, and criticized. God helped me to maintain interior charity and exterior calm; to deny or betray nothing, and yet not to irritate by too rigid assertions.

> But how much effort and interior distress this involves, and how necessary is divine grace to assist my weakness![24]

That this criticism still also involved her husband she reveals as she continued:

> My God, will You give me one day ... soon ... the immense joy of full spiritual communion with my dear husband, of the same faith and, for him, as for me, of a life turned toward You![25]

With her great sensitivity both to the promptings of the Holy Spirit and her discernment of the spiritual needs of others, her delicacy of soul was no better revealed than when she discerned that someone was searching for the truth. Such a one was her friend, Mme Vimont, and the correspondence that Félix published in his *Vie* is an excellent example of this. During her visits, it was obvious to Elisabeth that her friend was going through a period of great inner turmoil and anxiety, which Elisabeth recognised as being spiritual in nature. She was able to say with great certainty that 'I see clearly in you the work of divine grace. That anxiety which torments you is a "blessing", and the only thing I worry about is that at the end of the day it produces no fruit'.[26] She could see clearly that it was God's action that was causing her friend's inner darkness; it was a call to find him, and Elisabeth urged her not to let that call go unheeded. She sees Mme Vimont as a chosen soul, picked out to go through such a profound trial to make the choice for God. 'Yours has been given the dignity of that choice, and it does not astonish me to see it the prey of this trial of the Infinite, that profound anxiety which made St Augustine cry out, "Our hearts are made for you, O God, and they are restless until they rest in you".'[27]

She admits that although she can see clearly the cause, Elisabeth cannot see as clearly what her friend has to do to respond to that inner voice. Elisabeth, who has already gone through this process of discovering, and being discovered by, God, would love to take her friend over in one bound to the side of light and the clear air of heaven in which she herself breathes, and which gives her such happiness. However, she recognises that every call from God has its own timing and its own pace, and to hurry the process along can sometimes damage that delicate relationship which is unique to every person. Mme Vimont is searching, but that searching immediately throws up all her feelings of repugnance and hostility towards the faith that has kept her away from God in the first place. She does not want to be forced into doing something that she does not want to do.

Elisabeth assures her that God never forces a soul. The only time it seems there is pressure is when the light of truth suddenly becomes so clear and overwhelming that the soul is drawn into its ambience. Elisabeth, from the other side of that door, as it were, already in that light, knows how irresistible it is. 'In the measure that you seek and enter into it, the more luminous, the more beautiful, it will appear to you and you will be drawn more and more towards it.' Then, rather than being constricting, as her friend fears, 'it will be liberating, because the divine power will conquer you'.[28]

Besides her advice, Elisabeth offered her help in practical ways, by her suffering-enriched prayer, of course, by making available to Mme Vimont her extensive library of Catholic books, by suggesting a priest she might like to talk to and who would be sensitive to her needs.

When anyone came to her, or she went to someone whom she felt was open to the faith, her intention always was to 'work very humbly, very discreetly, effacing myself and disappearing as soon as the task is done, mixing no thought of self with the action performed by God alone'. Then, if she met with criticism, misunderstanding or prejudice, when she was misjudged, she would remind herself that Jesus himself was treated in the same way, 'and I will make myself as nothing in the eyes of others, I who am in fact so poor and little in the eyes of God'.[29] She was always acutely aware that she could be a catalyst, could be God's instrument in some small way, but it was God's grace alone that could effect the transformation. Nevertheless, it was a great joy to her whenever she 'discovered in someone resources that we did not expect, an instinctive need for the higher life, an unconscious seeking for the unknown God.' It would be all too easy to go in with too great an eagerness that might, even by a word which did not come from the Holy Spirit, destroy God's work in the soul. 'We must let Him speak, and we must show by our example and our lives alone the fulfilment of His deep and efficacious action in us.'[30]

More than anything, Elisabeth realised that she had to live a life that was Christian to the core and allow its beauty and its truth to draw others to desire what she possessed so abundantly.

This could have led to an artificial life, a striving to impress people by saying 'Look, how good I am!' This could always be a danger, but Elisabeth was so profoundly humble, so deeply aware that she was God's 'spoilt child', and that everything in her was his gift, that this danger did not arise. Being Christian was what she was, in her whole being, not a pose put on from the outside.

She knew through joyful experience that conversion can happen, and after the bitter aftertaste of conversations such as she had to endure in her social round, there came the news that a young Jewish woman convert was entering a Carmelite monastery. It was a reminder that God's grace could be active wherever there was a soul open to receive it; it gave her hope for the future, and the conviction that her prayer, taken up into the great mystery of the Communion of Saints, could be truly effective for the conversion of souls.

Notes

[1] E. Leseur, *My Spirit Rejoices* (Manchester: New Hampshire, Sophia Institute Press, 1996), pp. 64ff.
[2] *Ibid.*, p. 205.
[3] J. K. Ruffing RSM (edited, translated and introduced by), *Elisabeth Leseur* (New York: Classics of Western Spirituality, Paulist Press, 2005), p. 192.
[4] E. Leseur, *My Spirit Rejoices*, p. 29.
[5] *Ibid.*, p. 119.
[6] *Ibid.*, p. 120.
[7] *Ibid.*, p. 211.
[8] Ruffing RSM, *Elisabeth Leseur*, p. 300.
[9] *Ibid.*, p. 212.
[10] *Ibid.*, p. 213.
[11] *Ibid.*, p. 214.
[12] *Ibid.*, p. 193.
[13] *Ibid.*, p. 194.
[14] *Ibid.*, p. 201.
[15] *Ibid.*, p. 202.
[16] *Ibid.*
[17] *Ibid.*, p. 215.
[18] R. P. M.-A. Leseur (Félix Leseur), *Vie d'Elisabeth Leseur* (Paris: J. de Gigord, Editeur, 1946), p. 219.
[19] Ruffing RSM, *Elisabeth Leseur*, p. 220.
[20] *Ibid.*, p. 221.
[21] *Ibid.*, p. 30.
[22] *Ibid.*, p. 203.
[23] *Ibid.*
[24] E. Leseur, *My Spirit Rejoices*, p. 148.
[25] *Ibid.*
[26] M.-A. Leseur, *Vie d'Elisabeth Leseur*, p. 280.

[27] *Ibid.,* p. 281.
[28] *Ibid.,* p. 282.
[29] E. Leseur, *My Spirit Rejoices*, p. 175.
[30] *Ibid.,* p. 227.

5

WORK AMONG THE POOR

THE TURN OF the year of 1903 brought much happier times for Elisabeth, in her being able, personally, to take part in another conversion. In February, one of Félix's employees, a young man of about thirty, approached him to say that he wanted to be baptised. He explained that he had received no religious instruction, but that Providence had placed in his path a Dominican priest, Fr Hébert, who had converted him, given him instruction, and he now wanted to receive baptism. Félix, of course, was amused and surprised that any sane-minded person would voluntarily take such a step, saying,

'You want to be baptised? What a droll idea! But then, that's your affair.'

'I have to have a godmother,' the young man replied, undeterred, 'and I've come to ask if you would allow me to approach Mme Leseur, whom I know is very Catholic and practicing.'

Elisabeth, of course, was more than delighted to do this for him, and found one of their good Catholic friends to become his godfather. The ceremony was held in the crypt of the Dominican convent chapel of the Fauberg Saint-Honoré, 25 March, Feast of the Annunciation, although the Dominicans had been expelled from their convent a short while before. She wrote of that day:

> A fine morning, sweet and blessed! May God be praised for all the graces He has accorded me and for this great and supreme grace, for all that He has

ordained, and for leading my soul to a life wholly new and full of Him.[1]

It was all the sweeter for Elisabeth, because following this meeting Fr Hébert became her spiritual director; to some extent he filled the void and the need she had to be able to open herself out to someone who would understand her spiritual journey. It prepared her for an even deeper self-giving when she went with Félix to Rome for Holy Week in a pilgrimage organised by the Franciscan friars.

On the first Sunday there, 19 April, she received a card for an audience with Pope Leo XIII. After Mass, she set out with a friend to the Vatican and sat in the audience hall of the Court of St Damasus with other French pilgrims. She was near enough to the Pope to contemplate closely 'that thin, transparent face, full of intelligence and goodness. His eyes were unusual, full of life, suggesting his thoughtfulness and strong will. His soul radiated from those eyes'.[2] The Pope addressed them, and as he turned to go he leaned towards the pilgrims and made an emotion-filled gesture. Elisabeth looked at 'his beautiful face for the last time and said "good-bye" from the bottom of my heart, knowing that I would not see him again'.[3] The Pope did indeed die shortly afterwards, 20 July. She would recall that meeting some two years later when she wrote to Charles Duvent, thanking him for obtaining a blessing from the new Pope, Pius X. Charles had been invited to the Vatican to do a portrait of the new Pope, and during the sittings he spoke of Elisabeth and asked the Pope for a blessing for her. With her deep love and respect for the Papacy, Charles could not have given her a better gift. She told him of the indelible impression the previous Pope had made on her:

> I recall that almost transparent old man, clothed in white, with lively but profound eyes, with a noble gesture, his long transparent hand raised in bless-

ing; the acclamation of the crowd, and I experience once more the overwhelming sense I had at that moment. An inner happiness, an inexpressible sweetness, and I felt myself a member of that great living body which is the Church, of being united as one in that vast community, and a participation in that life which circulates in Christianity and, because of him, united in one same love, not only for those, like me, who are a part of the body of the Church, but of all those souls of good will.[4]

It is a testament to her greatness of soul that at a moment when Elisabeth could feel a sense of triumphalism in the heart of the Church and her sense of belonging, her vision was also caught by those people 'of good will' who are also, invisibly, a part of Christ's Body under the bonding headship of the Pope, even though they might not know it.

The following Wednesday she went alone to St Peter's. A French-speaking priest heard her confession, and she then received Communion in the Chapel of the Blessed Sacrament. Praying there, she had a profound experience of the living presence of Christ, of God, within her, conveying indescribable love:

> This blessed one spoke to me, and the infinite compassion of the Saviour passed quickly into me. Never will this action of God be effaced. The triumphant Christ, the eternal Word, He who as a human person suffered and loved, the one living God possessed my soul for all eternity in that unforgettable moment. I felt renewed in my very depths, ready for a new life, for responsibility, for the work intended by Providence. I offered myself and the future without reserve.[5]

How she would have loved afterwards to share this experience with Félix, but instead found herself returning to 'an atmosphere of irony, criticism, and indifference. But it was of no consequence, the flame of Christ was still burning within me'.[6] They spent the rest of Holy Week and Easter Sunday in Rome, then visited various churches, the catacombs and other ancient sites, before returning home to more trials.

It was difficult when she could not share the reason for her happiness and share that ineffaceable experience with those closest to her, especially Félix. She treasured the precious time of her morning meditation, her interior solitude with God alone, but isolation, so different from solitude, often weighed her down. She longed for sympathy, to be able to speak of her inner life, of God, of immortality, to someone else who really understood such things, and she never ceased praying for a day when that would happen:

> But the human soul is so subtle and delicate that it must feel the same notes resonating in another, of those divine instruments, before it can sound its own. The perfect union of two souls—how beautiful a harmony that would make! With him I love best in the world, let me one day make this harmony, O my God![7]

She did find in another priest, Abbé Viollet, someone with whom she could share something of her inner life. He had a keen, warm heart, able 'to understand what is of lasting value in Catholicism and that wonderful spiritual domain that so few know how to explore'.[8] After a talk with him in August she felt her energy renewed, encouraged to continue both her moral and material work, above all for those 'who are so mistaken and yet so interesting'. Her part was to have the same compassion for them that Christ has:

> To know how to understand them will be part of the task, to love them deeply will be another, but to love them for themselves alone and for God,

without any expectation of return or consolation, simply because they are persons and because Christ, in looking upon them one day, uttered this loving remark, 'I have compassion for the crowd' (Mark 8:2). Let us also know how to have mercy.[9]

Abbé Viollet's parents were close friends of the Leseurs, and he dined with them on occasion and spoke to them of the work he was doing in his parish. Besides being vicar of Notre-Dame-de-Rosaire de Plaisance, he had set up a dispensary installed by the Red Cross. One day in March the Leseurs went to visit him and to see it. In order to fund his various projects Abbé Viollet would organise musical and literary evenings, and he hoped the Leseurs, with all their contacts, would be interested in supporting him as well. Although Elisabeth did not want to get involved personally in that particular project, they did of course help him financially. Elisabeth herself was vitally concerned with the poor people who were becoming more and more marginalised due to the rapid industrialisation taking place in Europe, and the consequent exploitation of the workers.

In France there were great upheavals which were bringing the rights of the workers to greater attention. The Third Republic was established 4 September 1870, after the defeat of Napoleon III. This was followed by a popular uprising and the setting up of the revolutionary Paris Commune. It was quickly and bloodily crushed by Adolphe Thiers and in 1875 new constitutional laws were enacted. The Third Republic passed laws for the separation of Church and State, it recognised more rights for women, especially in their education, and in 1884 the right of workers to belong to trade unions was also recognised.

Many among the wealthy bourgeoisie remained royalists and yearned for the return of the monarchy and their old entitlements, but Elisabeth was not one of them. She felt that her class had a heavy responsibility toward the poor and that there was no way back from democracy. In this, she was greatly inspired by Pope Leo XIII's great encyclical *Rerum Novarum*, in which, for the first time, the Church acknowledged the rights of workers. There were also movements within Catholic circles in France to promote the rights of the poor and the workers. Elisabeth studied deeply the writings of Catholics who wrote and campaigned for them. For example, Charles de Montalembert, who often came into conflict with the Pope, but who nevertheless remained loyal to the Church. At an early age he exclaimed, 'Would it not be a splendid thing to show that religion is the mother of liberty!' which remained his motto throughout his life.

Joseph de Maistre was a staunch royalist, something he shared with Lacordaire, and was a supporter of the Jesuits. Elisabeth would not have agreed with many of his more extreme views of what could be called the 'divine right of kings' expressed in a broader sense, but she would have admired the beauty of his writing. There was Georges Goyau, who became a member and secretary of the Académie Française and an advocate of Social Catholicism, who called for 'a free Church in a free Europe'. After reading his books Elisabeth wrote to her sister Amélie:

> At least there are Catholics who are not hopeless and who do not believe in the restorative power of politics, but who preach the action of words and example. These are hard words, entirely appropriate for the sort of people known as conservative, a good word that deserves to be better applied. He says with reason that when one preaches the gospel to these people and demonstrates to them that society (their society) is anti-Christian, one seems to be revolutionary, and the 'good old times' for which they long are simply the time of privileges

and not that, even more distant time, when all classes were imbued with Christianity.[10]

There were some Catholics, like Albert de Mun, who set up workers' groups organized by the aristocracy for the people, and Léon Harmel, a factory owner who organised welfare services for his workers from the cradle to the grave. But on the whole the aristocracy were oblivious to their obligations.

If Elisabeth was disappointed with her own class and with many Catholics, she was equally scathing of the atheistic socialists and saw the limits of secular socialism, one of her maxims being, 'Socialism pretends to assure and transform the future; Christianity transforms the present'. She had no time for the various factions within the French Parliament and outside which were tearing each other apart with hatred for the other, while at the same time dreaming of establishing a universal brotherhood without establishing that brotherhood within their own hearts first. 'Politics deforms everything,' she wrote to Charles Duvent. It was no point in dreaming of universal love tomorrow without trying to put it into practice today. One blatant example of this woolly thinking was the Law of Associations. While proclaiming their intention to provide full equality of secular education, free from ecclesiastical control, for both girls and boys, they succeeded in closing down more than 10,000 schools run by the Church through its religious orders, without putting an equal alternative in its place. In the event, they had to re-open some 6,000 of them shortly afterwards, which were once again under religious control. Their vicious anti-clericalism drove them to try and abolish the very institutions that were providing the education that was needed.

Elisabeth was, of course, completely supportive of the new move towards equal education for girls, while decrying its wholly secular ethos, because for her, the most important task, the most urgent, was to reveal to people the idea of God.

She put her words into practice by setting up what she named 'Home for the Young Woman'. She recognised the need young women had for protection against the dangers of exploitation and prostitution in Paris, and in February 1903 rented a house in Vésinet, 12, rue du Chemin-de-Fer, near to the station. It was a large property with twelve rooms, set in a beautiful garden where the young girls could enjoy the peace and calm of their surroundings. They were required to pay a small monthly rent, since Elisabeth considered that things which were given for free were not appreciated. Because of the Law of Association banning religious organisations, she set it up as a purely philanthropic legal Association.

Because of her precarious health, Elisabeth had to measure her involvement, writing to Charles Duvent in October:

> I'm organising my days so that I am not too fatigued and above all to reserve my strength for the most important duties; in a month I hope to take up again my dear works which so sap my strength; I haven't gone to Charonne or Vésinet. Mme B in her goodness keeps me up to date from time to time as to what is happening. You can't believe the way we are spied on and subjected to surveillance, for fear that a nun in disguise doesn't slip in among the troops. It is going well and it is a great joy to me.[11]

She arranged for young girls, who were the most deprived yet who showed the most promise, to settle in the House and work for Worth, the famous dress designer of the time, and for the Syndicate of Needleworkers. For a time all went well. Mme Leduc, the dressmaker, reported that in a very short while the young workers were being transformed by their new surroundings, but the experiment was not to last.

Sadly, it failed, mostly from lack of funds and support, but also from the shortcomings of the lady in charge of it. She lacked initiative, but also did not understand the primary objectives for which Elisabeth had set it up. Further, it was too far from Paris for the girls to make the journey and keep in touch with their families, but there might have been another reason. Elisabeth herself always felt happiest in the countryside, where her health was best, and she felt invigorated by its peace and tranquillity. However, this might not have been the case with the young girls she invited to the Home, brought up as they were amid the bustle and vibrant life of Paris, however degrading it could also be, and perhaps they found life in the countryside too alien for their taste.

Elisabeth makes many references in her diary to her work for the poor. Félix and Elisabeth were wealthy and both were generous to those less fortunate than themselves. But Elisabeth's work for the poor went far deeper than philanthropy, and she pondered deeply on the social issues of her day in order to understand the best response to them. For her, her work for the poor started with the basics, that every single human being was a unique individual created by God. She was able to discuss her thoughts freely with Charles Duvent on all sorts of issues, knowing that they had a common understanding of the social problems of the day from the perspective of their Catholic faith. She explained her thought in a letter to him, while criticising the political movements she was observing:

> The Jaurès-Pressensé meeting had the same effect on us as it had on you. You see, politics distorts

everything it touches, and the electoral advertising forces us into awkward compromises! Certainly, I long passionately that more of peace and happiness would reign among men, but for that to happen we must start at the beginning. How can people who for the most part, hate each other, dream of establishing a universal brotherhood, without first making it live among themselves and in their own hearts? To constitute firmly and in union the family, this basis of humanity, then the homeland, and then, and only then, to seek to establish, more and more, peace and common effort among the peoples; this, it seems to me, is the truth. But to pursue a vague dream of universal love while squandering one's efforts on the common ground, and half opening the frontiers of the invasions of tomorrow, is folly! Let us seek between ourselves areas of agreement, working completely together for the common good.[12]

Elisabeth herself always sought those areas of agreement. Her whole social outlook was dominated by the conviction that the family was the basis of good governance, and therefore her efforts were mostly directed to helping, one on one, families who needed help to attain their full potential.

While she had eventually decided, reluctantly, to close her Home for the Young Women Elisabeth had other organisations to which she committed herself, and which were totally in accord with her way of thought. One of these was the Union Populaire Catholique, set up by a remarkable woman, Mlle Muller, who had devoted her life to the poor. She organised the work of the Union on two principles, first, that one should be actively engaged in the work on a personal level, and the second was to encourage the people with whom they worked to come to a greater knowledge, love and commitment to God. Each helper was assigned individual families that they would visit and give them all the help and support they could. The Union was active in the popular quarters and fauberges of Paris, among the most deprived and destitute, and had under its wing more than 2500 families. They helped the men to find work and ran training centres for them. They would help them with their rent, and ran a furniture store, libraries and classes and especially adult catechism courses. They set up holiday camps for the children in Juilly and Seine-sur-Marne.

The Union was divided into various sections, with each section being given considerable freedom and flexibility to adapt their activity to the various needs of the people in their area. Some would have a dispensary, in another they would run a restaurant, or a garden providing work for the men. On fixed days legal and medical centres would be open, with the doctors and lawyers giving their time free of charge. Whatever need there was, the Union tried to give it.

At the heart of all this activity was the Union's aim and work to bring the people back to God, and in this they had amazing success. Hundreds of children and adults were baptized, marriages performed or regularised, people brought back to the Faith. This primary aim was what appealed most profoundly to Elisabeth. She was assigned to a section of the Plaine-Saint-Denis, and she regularly visited the families assigned to her. She often tried to enthuse Félix with what she was doing, but with little success. He was keen on the overseas missions, but to Elisabeth's eyes there was far more poverty, moral and physical misery which appalled her, at the gates of Paris, than they had ever seen in their travels abroad. People needed to be raised out of their poverty by decent work, education and better health, by giving them hope for the future, so that they could see themselves as treasured children of God created for eternal life with him. This was Elisabeth's vision, and she approached the families under her care with her habitual delicacy, sensitivity and innate charm, embodying in herself what she was trying to bring to them for themselves. Mlle Mullet greatly appreciated these qualities in Elisabeth, which so matched her own, and there was a great affection and mutual respect between the two women.

Elisabeth was also closely involved in another, very similar organisation, the Union Familiale, set up in the Charonne quarter, one of the most deprived areas of Paris, by another woman of exceptional charity, Mlle Gahéry, described as having a strong will and outstanding intelligence, just the sort of person to whom Elisabeth would be drawn. Again, the Union was all-embracing in what it offered to the working men and women of the area. It set up classes for the young people and children, including summer camps, it taught them management skills and gave teacher training. The emphasis was on education—the women in household skills, young people on schooling, the men in best work practices.

Writing 1 August 1903, Elisabeth said that they had 'a lovely journey with the little ones. Contact is well-established among them, at least among some of them, and myself. I believe action is possible, but it is true to say that the workers failed the harvest. They need a good, intelligent will', adding that the work now included more than 300 families.[13] The ethos of the Union was deeply Catholic, and they ran catechism classes and other religious education schools, which led to an atmosphere of enthusiastic and intense religious life. There were 'neutral' areas for those who were not Catholic or religious, so that none were excluded, but the areas set aside for Christian education were organised in such an attractive way that the children of non-Catholic parents often begged for them to be allowed to join in.

Elisabeth worked with the smallest children, especially, under the direction of Mlle Gahéry, a work that so suited her maternal nature. She spoke of the work with enthusiasm to Félix, who had very little interest in it, but she was eventually able to persuade him to come with her and see for himself the sort of work that was being done. It was not a success; Félix saw the delight Elisabeth took in the work as she took him round and showed him everything. He saw the very real love she had for the children and the genuine affection and love they had for her, the influence she had over them by her calm and gentle firmness. They ate cakes in a restaurant that was popular with the Union, cakes that had been made in the catering school running a cookery class. But the poverty of the people, the barrenness of the surroundings, repelled him and he just could not understand the goodness and enthusiasm that Elisabeth visibly radiated. As they left, she asked Félix what his impressions were, and he responded with a grimace that expressed his disgust, remarking that 'Frankly, you know, I would prefer to go to the Rothschilds!'

Elisabeth smiled sadly, disheartened by Félix's response, but in her habitual gentle way replied, 'Don't say that. Suffering is the only thing of value here below; the day will come when the light will shine for you and you will understand. I pray daily that God will give you that grace'. Charles Duvent, on the other hand, had a great respect for Elisabeth and what he saw as her optimism, but she was quick to place the credit for this where it was due:

> You speak of my optimism, and what you call such is made up for me of many rough patches, great and small, of sacrifices and sadnesses; I well believe this name does not suit the condition you mean by it.

> Only—and I say this very humbly, because it is no merit of mine, but a grace—I have a very great and very precious resource. When human beings seem to me to be too wicked, that life and the effort that it calls for a little painful and duty arid; when I sense most keenly that there is in me something of the highest and the best, when I cannot find food for satisfaction in the midst of things and people who despise the good and ignore the beauty; then, I go to the source of all beauty and all truth; I take refuge there, in ardent prayer, close to him who gives the most profound peace; I console myself with the God of humanity and I return a little better and soothed about poor humans, my brothers.
>
> That is why, my dear friend, sorrowful as I so often am, like you, in this contact with the realities of life I cannot become bitter and scornful.[14]

Not that Elisabeth found it easy to walk among the ugliness of poverty, something that Duvent, as an artist appreciated. Writing to him Elisabeth brought up this aspect of her work:

> Yes, there is much evil, much meanness in the world, and the great error of the socialists and other reformers is to imagine that through violence, through the theories they develop, humanity will discover how to regenerate itself and enter into an era of endless happiness. These fine illusions last a long time, then comes the time of disillusionment and of discouragement, when one becomes pessimistic and gives up. This is all because the point of departure is false. Besides, as others as well as you have said, even the sincere exploit the situation. Even among the sincere there is often such arrogance, such a desire to play a role, to be the leader, and there is a subtle form of pride among the refined.[15]

She makes here the important point that true reform can never come through violence or be imposed from the outside. She herself could have fallen into the trap of coming in to the situation as a 'do-gooder', imposing her own ideas, but it is noteworthy that she worked under Mlle Gahéry and under her supervision in a subordinate position. As always, Elisabeth was acutely aware of the other person, no matter how poor, who had a dignity and a worth of their own, in whom God's grace was working; her role was to act as a catalyst if necessary, but above all being, herself, the best that she could be. In her letter to Charles, she continues:

> My dear friend, I am starting from a different point of view. I am persuaded that evil and suffering will never completely desert our poor earth, but I am also convinced that it is everyone's task to work to reduce evil and suffering as much as possible, in our own sphere, humbly, simply, without concern for our precious personality, through dedication, love, the gift of ourselves to that which is our duty. I believe that to accomplish this mission, the first thing to do is to try to become our best selves, even perhaps without knowing it. And God will do the rest. Our effort, our sacrifices, our actions, even the most hidden, will not be lost. This is my absolute conviction; everything has long-lasting and profound repercussions. This thought leaves little room for discouragement, but it does not permit laziness. We are poor day-labourers of life; we sow and God gives the harvest. You understand … I am unable to despair of humanity.[16]

So even, or perhaps most of all, her work among the poor was all part of her profound belief in the Communion of Saints, where every action, even the smallest and most hidden, when done in love, has eternal repercussions. As she said, 'one act of goodness raises the whole world'. Also, when her health began to give way and she was less and less able to take on active work, she had the vivid assurance that her prayer, her suffering, was of immense value for those whom she sought to serve. She would still have her apostolate, but in a different form. Nothing was wasted in the eyes of God.

It was difficult for Elisabeth to move from this work among the poorest, to the circles where she and Félix would be completely at home calling on the Rothschilds. There she found a different sort of poverty, a poverty of spirit, of shallowness and what she called frivolity. She saw them as children, and equally in need of her love:

> I must nevertheless know how to make myself all things to all men and interest myself in things that sometimes seem childish, and which sadden me by their contrast with my own state of mind. Often people are like great children, but Jesus has said that what is done for children is done for Him. So let us show indulgence to childishness and to the incredible light-mindedness of so many about us, and insofar as it is useful, let us learn how to become little with all types of 'little ones', even the little of soul. Let us try to speak the language they can understand, and with them stammer eternal truths. Has not God done the same with us, and has He not placed in our souls only as much light as we can bear?[17]

She had no contempt for these people, especially the women, who had no real aim in life apart from the social whirl; perhaps because at that time so many outlets were closed to them apart from socialising. They were just as needy, and her love and compassion embraced them, too; they, no less than the poor, needed to be given an inkling of the eternal destiny to which they were called. Where

Elisabeth felt there might be someone who was even a little open to the message of the Gospel, she would, with her inborn tact and delicacy, discern what they might need in the way of encouragement. She shared books from her well-stocked library, giving them away freely if she felt they might be of help.

Although she recognised that when she moved among upper-class circles she had to dress accordingly, she decided that this did not prevent her from dressing more modestly and simply, which was surely more in keeping with her character, anyway. Félix, in his love for her, would shower her with gifts, but as she became more engrossed in her social work she was able to persuade him to give her the money instead, so that she could spend it on her charitable works.

There was one gift, however, that she accepted with profound love. This was a beautiful little writing desk Félix gave her, a gift to express his sorrow when one day he realised that he had hurt her deeply. Félix, to denigrate her faith, nicknamed her Mme Péchin, a character from the novel by Anatole France, 'The Amethyst Ring', who believed in eternal life, to which the agnostic doctor Fornerol responds, 'but you are not at all immortal. You will last no longer than the stars … But you are not at all immortal Madam Péchin'. Under this provocation, Elisabeth would say nothing and usually bore these attacks with good humour and a smile, but on this occasion he recognised that he had gone too far and really hurt her. He gave her the little bureau with a love letter attached, and Elisabeth was overwhelmed, writing in her diary:

> Some joyful days because of a present from Félix, and more because of the words that accompanied it—words so full of love that made me very happy. I do not deserve to be so loved, but I rejoice fully

in it. Apart from the love that is the very foundation of my life, I am always meeting with wonderful affection, for thus has God blessed me.[18]

Her first use for the desk was to write a note to her husband, sending 'from the depth of my little Péchin heart a feeling of tenderness, in which all forms of love are mixed together, united so that it would be impossible to separate them'.

As the entry to her diary shows, she could not separate the love she bore, especially towards her husband, the one she loved most of all on earth, towards her family and friends, from the love that God had poured so abundantly into her heart.

Elisabeth was unable to have children herself, but she had the heart of a mother, but she was able to use that maternal love God had given her to pour out her love on her family and friends, into her work among the poor, which became a love that embraced the whole world.

Notes

[1] E: Leseur, *My Spirit Rejoices* (Manchester, New Hampshire: Sophia Institute Press, 1996), p. 70.
[2] J. K. Ruffing RSM (edited, translated and introduced by), *Elisabeth Leseur* (New York: Classics of Western Spirituality, Paulist Press, 2005), p. 69.
[3] Ibid., p. 70.
[4] R. P. M.-A. Leseur (Félix Leseur), *Vie d'Elisabeth Leseur* (Paris: J. de Gigord, Editeur, 1946), p. 232.
[5] Ruffing RSM, *Elisabeth Leseur*, p. 70.
[6] Ibid.
[7] E. Leseur, *My Spirit Rejoices*, p. 62.
[8] Ruffing RSM, *Elisabeth Leseur*, p. 71.
[9] Ibid., pp. 70ff.
[10] Ibid., pp. 21ff.
[11] M.-A. Leseur, *Vie*, p. 261.

[12] *Ibid.,* p.252.
[13] *Ibid.,* p. 265.
[14] *Ibid.,* p. 158.
[15] Ruffing RSM, *Elisabeth Leseur,* pp. 165ff.
[16] *Ibid.*
[17] E. Leseur, *My Spirit Rejoices*, p. 89.
[18] *Ibid.,* pp. 56ff.

6

JULIETTE

ELISABETH WAS FORCED by circumstances to put her social work on hold for a while when the family was told that her sister, Juliette, had become seriously ill with tuberculosis. In the autumn of 1903 her health had begun to give them concern, and in an entry in her diary for 3 November Elisabeth writes of the toll the anxiety for her sister was having on her, which was added to her own ill health. She spoke of a little-mentioned aspect of an incurable illness such as hers: she would have to come to terms with the fact that her illness would be life-long and the strain it would put on the spirit to cope with that understanding. Elisabeth was also concerned that it was preventing her from doing all she wanted in her charitable work and the other obligations of her life. Still, the New Year brought her a reminder of what she so longed for, bringing souls to God, when she met the little girls of the Charonne who were making their First Communion. Those were the souls in which she could sow the seed, leaving the harvest to God.

Easter that year was also a time of joy, contrasted with a few months previously when Elisabeth had said that her inner state was that of being without joy or consolation. With the celebration of Easter it was as if she had been given a new lease of spiritual life, a new beginning, which she needed in the face of Juliette's increasing illness and all the difficulties that brought for the whole family. It was especially hard for her mother, who had already lost one daughter and her husband, and was now faced with the certainty of losing another daughter. For Elisabeth, her strong faith bore witness to the paradox of the Christian life, that in the midst of suffering there is also peace:

> And yet through all these trials and in spite of the lack of interior joy, there is in my soul some central place, which all these waves of sorrow cannot reach. In this place is hidden all my inner life; there I can feel how completely united I am to God, and I regain strength and serenity in the Heart of Christ.[1]

Juliette had never married and being five years younger than Elisabeth, from their earliest years Elisabeth had been like a little mother to her; Juliette had been the 'child of her heart' and the friend of her soul. She was also like a sister to Félix, who loved her very dearly. He described her as an exquisite woman, with a cultivated intellect and a happy and spiritual character. If she had not been so unaffectedly good, he said, she would have been easily brilliant, with a fine critique and incisive repartee. But her deep piety took away any superficial brilliance that could hurt others and imprinted on her whole being a most attractive gentleness and sweetness, without detracting from her fine mind. Félix was able to enjoy speaking with Juliette of her literary and artistic tastes which conformed to his. During the holidays the family spent together she made a delightful and pleasant companion with her unfailing good humour and her love of life.

Sadly, Juliette had been able to enjoy a stay in Jougne only in 1902 and 1903; in 1904 she was too weak to join them. Instead, she and her mother, who was also unwell, stayed in Versailles with the Durons. Amelie also remained in Paris for three weeks, so the stay at Jougne in July was a scattered affair. Elisabeth looked after the children there and she was happy that Félix could also be with them, although he was called away for a short while to Chateau-

Thierry where his mother was ill with severe phlebitis. Elisabeth wrote to Duvent telling him all this news, adding:

> My heart is with my dear little invalid all the time, and my life is but a prayer for her. Dear friend, in the sad hours of life, there are only two things true and strengthening: the dear affections which help to bear suffering, and God who gives to suffering an explanation and a reward; among these affections of which I speak, yours and mine, yours, once again have done good for me.[2]

In the autumn Juliette felt a little better and went to Passy, where her mother rented an apartment which was perfect for her, very airy and sunny, with a superb view of the Bois de Boulogne.

Elisabeth had a great joy in October when she went with Félix to Moulins where he had a lawsuit; she was able to slip away one afternoon while he was in the law courts, to visit Paray-le-Monial and the shrine of St Margaret Mary who had received the revelations of devotion to the Sacred Heart, a devotion that was very dear to Elisabeth.

She took up her normal routine on their return to Paris in September, and in her diary she noted how her desires had matured and deepened. She wanted to be a Christian, an apostle, and to her the two were inseparable. She wanted to be a Christian to her very depths, to her very core. Time and again in her diary she describes how she found that the sacrament of Confession and of receiving the Eucharist had tangible effects on her, restoring her peace and strengthening her:

> On Wednesday I had a striking example of what God's grace can do, and I saw how abundantly it is given in the sacraments. I had spent the morning in a state of extreme prostration and sadness; during the day I went to confession, and I was at peace

again; I seemed to be—and indeed I was—renewed by a strength other than my own. The sense of forgiveness and spiritual renewal in the sacrament of penance is wonderful. And yesterday morning I received communion with the same peace and the same abandonment to God. I felt Jesus truly living in me, and now I want to become different, to be totally Christian, with all that that word means of self-forgetfulness, strength, serenity and love.[3]

Besides the charitable organisations that worked among the poor which Elisabeth supported and worked for, she was also a committed member of an association for women, set up in 1903, to spread Eucharistic adoration. Their aim was to be 'living hosts' that allowed the Saviour to live fully in them in order to shed his light on those around them. This fully accorded with Elisabeth's own apostolate and her love for the Eucharist. The association was founded in response to Pope Pius X's desire that Catholics should receive communion frequently, a practice that until then had not been common. The association had published a little book entitled 'Let us be Apostles', which set out their teachings and which provided daily meditations. Elisabeth was so helped by it that she kept a copy by her bedside and bought copies to distribute as widely as she could. It had been published anonymously but was written by the foundress of the association, Mme Ricard, who, when she heard how enthusiastically Elisabeth was distributing her book, hoped very much to meet her. The two of them met eventually when she came to Paris in 1911 or 1912. Elisabeth made a profound impression on her by her charm and deep spirituality.

Visiting her sister often, Elisabeth could see how Juliette was also growing spiritually as her illness progressed. One of the sufferings Elisabeth endured was that she was unable to share her inner life with those closest to her, but now in Juliette she found she could, to the sister whom she said had a soul 'fairer and loftier than my own'. Even at the time of her First Communion at the age of twelve, Juliette had remarked, to her family's astonishment, 'there is no need to fear death, because then we will find God again!' The times Elisabeth spent with her sister were among the best of her life, as she notes in her diary:

> This dear woman moves and inspires me more than I can say. I love her soul, and I think she understands mine. This is a great consolation because, of those who surround me, apart from Maman, my sisters, and my dear Félix, no one knows my inner self.[4]

Félix and Elisabeth's mother may have known of her inner life to a certain extent, but they were unable truly to understand the real depths of it.

With the turn of the year Juliette became more seriously ill, and Elisabeth spent nearly all her time at her bedside. She herself suffered cruelly as she witnessed Juliette's sufferings, but they were also able to talk of things that were closest to their hearts. Writing to her friend Aimée Fiévet, she said that her sister, after receiving Holy Communion, said, 'in a tone of voice I will never be able to forget, "I love him, and I have abandoned myself to him"'.[5]

Like Elisabeth, Juliette was offering her sufferings for Félix's conversion. Elisabeth recounted the last conversation Félix had with Juliette shortly before her death:

'Do you know what I have been doing while you weren't here?' Juliette asked him.

'No', he replied, though he knew perfectly well.

'Well, I received extreme unction, and I offered some of it for you.' Félix was deeply moved and tried to hide his emotion, asking her wistfully, 'So you don't find me very good?'

Juliette replied with inexpressible gentleness that she recognised that with all his goodness, with all his sterling qualities, there were some that remained unused. Elisabeth had obviously discussed with her sister her prevision that her husband would eventually become a priest and which Félix knew about and he replied, 'So don't you want me to become a priest?'

Elisabeth, hiding her own emotion and trying to make light of it, said, 'So that's it, he'll become a priest when he becomes a widower!'[6]

They were all praying fervently that she would be cured, but it was not to be. She died with her eyes fixed on Elisabeth, who had 'the terrible sorrow' of closing them and of kissing her for one last time.

Elisabeth wrote to Aimée that, outwardly, her sister had achieved nothing here below, that her vibrant soul had had 'every noble aspiration without being able to fulfil it'. However, in the spiritual realm she had attained, Elisabeth was convinced, the highest 'achievement' there could be, dying as a saint, 'her ultimate flowering, and the true life, which we only begin in this world and that we get glimpses of in our better moments, those when we unite ourselves with that which is infinite and eternal'.[7] Juliette had accepted her suffering and her death, loving and praying, and had turned them into a treasure of infinite worth.

So deeply did Elisabeth feel her loss that in the entry in her diary for that day, all she could set down was the date, 13 April 1905, with a cross beneath it. It was not until July that she was at last able to put her thoughts in writing, to express her anguish at her loss, but also the firm hope she had that her beloved sister was now in the presence of God. If she had been denied earthly happiness, then:

> It is because a better life awaited her on the other side. The God of love prepared her for a joy beyond

> her suffering, and God wanted her to enjoy all good and beauty and to give her his light; and that her dear soul was purified and holy so that she could approach the holiness of God.[8]

Elisabeth felt shattered, but part of her remained with her sister, in the presence of God, and her conviction of the reality of the Communion of Saints was deepened and enriched. This understanding was not only that she had the prayer of her sister to support her, but also that her own prayer here on earth was efficacious for souls, both for those on earth and those in purgatory. When she received the sacraments, especially Holy Communion, then she was united with the whole Church, and the graces she received through them enriched the whole world.

She expressed this same thought to her mother-in-law, who wrote to her in November for her name day of St Elisabeth:

> Let me thank you from the bottom of my heart for your motherly wishes and even more for your prayers. It is the best present you could give me, what I desire the most, above all when, and it is the case for you, these prayers extend to our dear Félix. I have asked our sisters, [Juliette and Mme Leseur's daughter Claire] as a present for the feast day, to obtain for us that which we wish so much for him, and to make of him the admirable Christian as I firmly hope, that he could and will be. On my feast day, which I expected would hold so much sorrow for me, he spoke to me most tenderly of Juliette and the recollections he has of her, and I told him how much I love you and the others I love, and how much I am united with my dear departed ones. They will be, and already are, the unseen protectors of that soul whom we love, and they will obtain for

him that light which God gives so quickly, if he wills, and which he alone can give.[9]

This letter gives a touching insight into the relationship Elisabeth had with her mother-in-law and the closeness of the bonds that bound all their families at that time above all. Mme Leseur must have been in continual sadness for the son who had so completely abandoned the faith of his upbringing, but she would have been consoled by her daughter-in-law's strong faith in the Communion of Saints and the power of prayer to obtain his eventual conversion.

Elisabeth also tried to encourage her own mother, who understandably was equally devastated by the loss of her daughter, to have a like understanding that Juliette was still present to her, though unseen. In one of her letters to her mother she described how she went to the little oratory she had made in her bedroom, full of the thoughts of the day Juliette died, her heart heavy and broken:

> And then, dear mother, I had been praying for her for only a few moments, and yet more, with her, for you and for myself, when, like a gentle response from her who would not see us sad, I was filled with a peace that transformed my inner vision and brought back to me all the sweetness of memories, with a sense of the blessedness of our dear one. I felt her so close, that we were surrounded by her protection which we could discern if we set aside all that could trouble that sweet union of souls; I truly felt much stronger then.[10]

The return from Jougne in October was even more difficult for her, back to her life in Paris, her work among the poor, with all its pressures and trials, as she wrote to Duvent:

> After a holiday in Jougne, in great repose of soul and body, the return here has been painful for me.

> To take up again normal existence without the dear one who filled it seems to me to be a task that is almost too much for my strength. So I don't rely on it and I abandon myself entirely to that fatherly Providence who has never let me down. And yet again, he has sustained me; for through all the sorrow, through all my frequent physical miseries, I am able to rest intimately united to the divine will. As I said to Juliette, I want to 'reform my life', that is to say, without any great external changes and without ever making myself conspicuous, to establish strongly in my soul more of serenity, true humility, and charity. I also want to be true more and more, and that is more difficult than it seems.[11]

She may have felt shattered, but she was determined to continue with her work in serenity and even in joy, however much it cost her and however much she felt she failed at times. Félix could not help but notice that the trials she had gone through and the courage with which she faced them, was having a profound effect on her character. If, externally, she continued to carry out her work wonderfully as a woman of the world, it was no longer her main concern; that concern was, in a word, to carry out without reserve the will of God, accepting and offering to him her suffering, her devotion to her neighbour and the sanctification of her soul. She had overcome herself, conquered all her hastiness of temper, acquiring an equilibrium of joy and kindness and a serenity that would never henceforth leave her. She considered that joy and laughter were essential for Christians, and loved St Teresa of Avila for these qualities; Teresa, who had proclaimed that she had no time for sad saints. Only Félix, who was closest to her, was able to discern the effort it took her sometimes and could see the sadness behind the smile.

Félix was also able to discern that all this was due to her deep faith, which he did not share but which he now came grudgingly to respect; so much so that he began to soften his attacks on her faith, which he recognised meant so much to her.

The trial of Juliette's illness and death had purified them both in the fire of suffering. Elisabeth could not believe that Juliette's suffering had no purpose or meaning, and shortly afterwards, she put into words her Credo, what she firmly believed about suffering, which she had seen and experienced in herself so much, and the Communion of Saints, which was linked vitally to her understanding of redemptive suffering.

> I believe that suffering was accorded by God to man with great intention of love and mercy.
> I believe that Jesus Christ has transformed and sanctified suffering and made it almost divine.
> I believe that suffering is the great instrument of redemption and sanctification for the soul.
> I believe that suffering is fruitful, as much as and sometimes more than our words and deeds, and that the hours of Christ's Passion did more for us and were more powerful with the Father than even His years of preaching and earthly activity.
> I believe that there is coursing through souls—those on earth, those in Purgatory, and those who have attained to true life—a great unending stream made up of the sufferings, merits and love of all these souls, and that our least sorrow, our faintest efforts can, by divine action, reach certain souls, whether near or far, and bring them light, peace, and holiness.
> I believe that in eternity we shall find again the beloved ones who have known and loved the Cross, and that their sufferings and our own will be lost in the infinity of divine Love and the joy of final reunion.
> I believe that God is love, and that suffering, in His hand is the means used by His love to transform and save us.

I believe in the Communion of Saints, the resurrection of
the body, and life everlasting.[12]

This time of suffering brought all the family even closer
together, none more so than Elisabeth and Félix. She wrote
a few poems at this time, one of them in response to a gift
from her husband of a paper weight enclosing a purple
butterfly:

> It is purple, a shade somewhat sad,
> Like my heart.
> In my heart there always remains
> A sadness.
> But that shade is hot and strong
> Like my heart,
> To which your dear love gives
> So much sweetness.[13]

She wrote him another, longer, poem a year later, when
to their great delight and pride he was nominated as a
Chevalier of the Legion of Honour. She wrote in it that
her heart was filled with tenderness, pure pride and joy,
but she also pointed out that he now wore one cross for
the two of them. He wore the cross of the Legion of
Honour given for his work and his valour, while the cross
she wore was for her pains and previous efforts:

> But God triumphant whom I adore with my whole being
> Places before my weary eyes the crucifix.
> May the unclouded and happy cross always shine on the days
> made up of work and exquisite goodness,
> Then, when I die, place on my grave
> The other Cross, which is my love and my only boast.[14]

Notes

[1] E. Leseur, *My Spirit Rejoices* (Manchester, New Hampshire: Sophia Institute Press, 1996), p. 81.
[2] R. P. M.-A. Leseur (Félix Leseur), *Vie d'Elisabeth Leseur* (Paris: J. de Gigord, Editeur, 1946), p. 166.
[3] J. K. Ruffing RSM (edited, translated and introduced by), *Elisabeth Leseur* (New York: Classics of Western Spirituality, Paulist Press, 2005), p. 78.
[4] *Ibid.*
[5] *Ibid.*, p. 209.
[6] B. Chovelon, *Élisabeth et Félix Leseur* (Paris: Groupe Artège, 2015), pp. 127ff.
[7] *Ibid.*, p. 208.
[8] *Ibid.*, p. 80.
[9] M.-A. Leseur, *Vie d'Elisabeth Leseur*, p. 278.
[10] *Ibid.*, pp. 177ff.
[11] *Ibid.*, p. 178.
[12] E. Leseur, *My Spirit Rejoices*, pp. 235ff.
[13] R. P. M.-A. Leseur, *Vie d'Elisabeth Leseur*, p. 379.
[14] *Ibid.*, p. 380.

7

TREATISES FOR HER NEPHEW AND NIECE

A MONTH AFTER JULIETTE'S death, Marie, Elisabeth's niece, made her First Communion. Juliette had been named as her godmother and had so longed to be there for the great day, but it was not to be. Realising this, Juliette had asked Elisabeth to take her place, something that she agreed to with all her heart, for Marie was almost like the daughter to her that she could never have.

During the weeks and months that Elisabeth had spent by her sister's bedside they had talked of many things concerning the spiritual life, and Elisabeth had put down the most important thoughts in writing, reading them over to her sister, often in tears and with great emotion. They were the 'Little Treatise on Hope' and the 'Little Treatise on Peace'. She now copied them out as two booklets for Marie to keep as a souvenir of her First Communion and also as a remembrance of her two aunts.

They were too advanced, perhaps, for Marie to understand as an eleven-year old, but she treasured them; she had now become, in Juliette's place, the 'child of her heart' and who, Elisabeth hoped, would become her friend as she grew up. The treatises reveal much of the inner thoughts that so united Marie's aunts in those last months of Juliette's life.

Elisabeth wrote a covering letter that went with the treatises, and she explains how she had come to write them. If Félix had discerned the profound changes in Elisabeth, then she, too, had recognised what the grace of God had worked in her, 'a love so fatherly that I am able to believe in Divine Providence after seeing it, so to speak, at work in my life and heart'. She had also seen it at work powerfully in her beloved sister, which gave her added confidence in her own eternal destiny. Despite her grief, her worries, and her ill health, which could have plunged her into darkness, she wrote:

> The great, true sun has risen above the horizon of my soul, and all the clouds of suffering fail to obscure its brightness, while it has tinged them with its divine radiance. My wish is to live and die in its light, veiled now so that our poor mortal eyes may endure it; but I look forward to the full glory of that light in eternity, when I shall be reunited with those whom we have loved so dearly and shall love forever.[1]

In her little treatise Elisabeth says that this Christian hope is totally different from ordinary, earthly hope or a natural instinct that is based on what is passing and ephemeral, 'influenced by circumstances apart from itself' or a pleasant anticipation. The Scriptures describe hope as an anchor (Heb 6:19), Christ within us is our hope of glory and our assurance (Col 1:27, Heb 6:11), it is a living hope (1Pt 1:3). It is a gift from God we can ask him for, which we must prepare ourselves to receive and be actively working with when received. It is vitally linked with the other virtues of faith and charity, and as the word 'virtue' implies, it is a strength given to the soul. Because it is a divine gift, when a word is spoken in the strength of divine hope, then it gives genuine encouragement to those broken, sad or bereaved, because 'our poor words derive all their efficacy from the Eternal Word'.

Because it is a divine gift it gives 'to our souls that strength and serenity which will be the light of our lives, and will completely transform our souls, the world, and life itself in our own sight'.[2]

Elisabeth possessed abundantly the virtue of hope, and the strength and serenity it gave was powerful and visible in her. Because she was writing the treatise in the light of Juliette's death, she could say:

> We know that nothing is lost, either in the material or spiritual world, and that the lowliest of our actions, the most secret of our prayers, has immeasurable force, for it echoes on through time and space, and it may be that, ages hence, some human hearts may be brought into mysterious contact with us.[3]

This is a wonderful, boundless vision which is true because it belongs to the Communion of Saints, where all are vitally linked into the Body of Christ in the bonds of undying and unshakeable love and is unbounded by space and time. Because of that, it is down to earth and practical, affecting those we meet or even those unknown to us:

> Let us seek them, understand them, and love them, from the soul of the maidservant in our house, and those that are shrouded sometimes under a ridiculous or gloomy exterior; to those distant and unknown souls that can nevertheless be affected by our prayers and sufferings, although it is only in eternity that they will learn how our passing sorrows or our humble sacrifices have won for them life everlasting.[4]

In this passage Elisabeth describes the inner springs from which she goes out in love to the poor people she serves in her charitable work, the love and compassion she has for the often frivolous and shallow people, poor in spiritual things, she met through the social functions she attended, in the circles to which she belonged, in her own household and family.

Christian hope also sheds light and gives understanding about suffering, death, the problems and hardships we meet on earth, as well as the assurance of the life after death that Christ has revealed to us.

> It puts us into closer union with God and extends our view into that wonderful region of souls which faith first opens to us, and which charity allows us to penetrate fully. It is a region never entered by those who live on the surface of things, and yet it is free to every Christian.[5]

In her 'little treatise' on peace Elisabeth reveals more of herself and the serenity that was such a marked aspect of her character. As with hope, the peace that Jesus gives and which was a gift he gave to his disciples on the eve of his Passion and death, is not of this world (John 14:27), is not therefore dependent on external circumstances, and does not depend on having no external worries or concerns. That is why Elisabeth discovered that even the death of Juliette, her worries over her mother's health, the battle she had with her own health, even her periods of spiritual darkness, could not disturb that peace and joy she found deep with herself:

> God alone is the author of all peace, and therefore it is of Him that we must ask for peace day by day. If we relied on ourselves to obtain peace we would soon be disappointed. Each day is made up of little complications, little annoyances and trifling duties, and unless we bring order into this confusion, we shall soon be overwhelmed and lose our moral balance.[6]

It is a peace that the lowliest can and ought to know. It is therefore in the little things of daily life where we can learn peace and little by little establish ourselves in unshakeable peace, which will give us strength and the resources we need when greater trials come our way. Although she does not touch on it in this treatise, Elisabeth was well aware that it was also these little duties of everyday life that must be offered up to God as expressions of love, which, because they are done in love, and love is the basis and whole ambience of life in God, have eternal consequences.

Peace is given above all through the sacraments, especially Communion and Confession, and enables us to keep near to souls for their healing; in this way it makes us apostles:

> We must keep near to the souls God puts in our way and try to understand and love them. Here we have discovered, by God's grace, the sources of peace and the means of possessing it fully.[7]

So fully did the people around her experience this peace and tranquillity that emanated from her, that Félix Le Dantec would tell his wife Yvonne, when she became upset and anxious, 'So go and see Elisabeth, go and take a bath in her serenity'. It is the companion of joy, and the two are inseparable, even in the midst of suffering, and Elisabeth notes how often joy is mentioned in the Scriptures. That is why she asked that the joy and laughter that were always on her lips and in her face would also penetrate into her soul. It allows the Christian to repeat with St Paul that 'I live, now not I, but Christ lives in me' (Gal. 2:20). 'We have all met persons of this sort', she says, undoubtedly thinking of such friends as Mlle Muller, Mlle Ricard and Mlle Gahéry. That this was also true of Elisabeth herself is revealed in a passage in which she gives a description which beautifully describes her own self:

> They are rare, no doubt, but there flows from them such an intensity of inner life, such calm strength, such true beauty that merely to come into contact

with them soothes and comforts us. After all, this is only natural. Our outer life is the reproduction of our inner life, and the visible part of us reflects what is unseen; we radiate our souls, so to speak, and, when they are centres of light and warmth, other souls need only to be brought into contact with them in order to be warmed and enlightened. We give out, often unknown to ourselves, what we carry within us; let us strive to increase daily this reserve store of faith and quiet charity.[8]

Elisabeth also wrote another treatise for Marie herself, 'Christian Womanhood', in which she describes the aspirations and the goals of a Christian woman. She did not envisage a career for Marie, since at that time women were only just beginning to be admitted to universities, and careers were not something women of their social class were expected to follow. She foresaw for Marie what she herself had been called to, marriage, and for her niece, children. In this, Elisabeth saw the greatest calling, because Marie, as wife and mother, would be developing and forming the next generation. For her, the family was the vital and indispensable building block of society, and within the family unit the woman was most involved in nurturing the children, forming their characters both for their place in the world and as Christians.

If this was the woman's role, then Marie could not pass on what she did not herself have. Moving in her social circle, Elisabeth was grieved at the shallowness of so many of her women friends and acquaintances, at their intellectual and spiritual poverty. By contrast, Elisabeth herself never ceased to educate herself, learning languages, never losing her keen interest on what was going on in the world, reading to improve her understanding of the social changes that were happening in France and beyond, reading to deepen her understanding of her Catholic faith. She felt that this was the duty of every woman, and in her 'treatise' to Marie encouraged her to follow in her aunt's footsteps.

For Elisabeth, being a wife and a mother was not a second-choice vocation, whose work was mostly done when her children had attained adulthood. It was a lifelong and vital commitment to society. From the home, Marie should reach out to others in the same social class in which they both moved, in the charitable works that were such an important part of Elisabeth's own vocation as a Catholic lay person. At the basis of all this was the conviction that each person was put on the earth by God to do some good, a good that would reverberate to future generations.

As Christians, we might seem no different from others, but a Christian has another dimension to the outwardly-seeming ordinariness of her life, because she has the light of faith:

> This light of faith proceeds directly from God, and forms the supernatural existence, bestowing on our actions, although they apparently resemble those of other people, an aim that others have not, and an incomparable value to ourselves and souls. As beings possessed of sense and reason, we live lives that differ in no respect from that of the other members of the human race, but there is something beyond, which is not, as too many people suppose, antagonistic to this life.[9]

In this last remark she touches upon an accusation often made by the atheist, and which she had often heard among her atheist friends and her own husband, that faith diminishes a person and has no place among the scientific, rationalist and materialist new world of the present age. Not so, Elisabeth says adamantly. Faith brings together in a harmonious whole within the person both the spiritual and the rational aspects of the human person. 'There is no peculiarly Christian kind of learning,' she says. 'Learning is the same for all, whether they are believers or not,' but a Christian has an added dimension to life, by which she can 'reach those mysterious realities that constitute man in his entirety'. So:

> A Christian is, therefore, in one sense complete, for his thought and action may be as wide as that of the greatest scholar—depending on his intellectual faculties—and at the same time, the sphere of the infinite and eternal lies open to him, revealing not only the world of sense, the knowledge of the changes and events that take place, but also the infinitely greater and unchanging world of God and the human soul.[10]

The implication is, then, that it is the atheist, by denying this other dimension of the human person, who is narrow and confined in his outlook, rather than the Christian.

The confrontation with atheism is a theme she picks up in the treatise she wrote a year later for her nephew, André Duron, for his First Communion. Again, it was a treatise that looked forward to the time when, as a young man and no longer a child, he would take his place in society. She had only the one niece but more nephews, so she intended this treatise to be for them also as they grew up.

She begins the treatise with the death of Juliette, still very present in all their minds and the thought that we are, first of all, citizens of heaven before being citizens of the world. She wants the graces of André's First Communion to endure and be the bedrock of whatever path of life he chose later on. In this, and speaking from her own experience, prayer would be indispensible and would give him the stability he would need to live a truly Christian life:

> To pray is to live in constant, calm, strong and lasting union with God, to look at everything from

God's point of view, and to be so peacefully anchored in eternity that annoyances, unavoidable struggles and continual activity have no ability to disturb us or to drag us down.[11]

Among these struggles would be the inevitable meeting with those who were not Christian and who indeed were anti-Christian, and who would try to rob him of his faith. There would be the temptation to water down or even abandon his faith. To counter this, André should build up spiritual reserves and conviction, 'of humble, confident faith, of intense charity and kindness'.

She again draws on her own experiences, which cut her to the quick, of the 'terrible thing that few resist—sarcasm. To be able to stand firm despite the disdainful smile is a sign of great moral strength'.

When Elisabeth studies her own faith, she seeks to have responses to the challenges thrown down by the atheist, but she sees deeper than this. That faith must be embedded profoundly within a person, it must be what that person really is. It is imbibed from the outside, as it were, but must not remain there. As Elisabeth herself said, it was to be Christian to the core. Even then, there is more. The Christian faith is not a series of propositions that one accepts and makes one's own. It is meeting a person, Jesus Christ, and being incorporated into the very life of God himself, the Most Holy Trinity. The propositions introduce the Christian to that life of God and make it a reality. In her prayer, Elisabeth would study, read the Gospels, receive the sacraments, because it was there that she met Christ and became more and more profoundly united to him, and this is what she wanted for André, and indeed for everyone.

When he leaves school to study for a career André will find himself in an atmosphere of unbelief which will make him feel 'uncomfortable in the atmosphere of faith'. The only remedy is to have what she calls, following St Teresa of Avila, 'experimental knowledge' of God. It is not enough to have outward observance without inward conviction. It is to 'pray and to work'. André must give prayer priority in his life, together with a good work ethic that would express and give shape to his inner life, so that people, who had no knowledge of Christianity, would see it made visible in his life.

She takes his life even further and looks ahead to his old age, when other avenues of service to others may no longer be possible, but the vocation of prayer and intercession is always possible, especially at the end of life when he would be constrained by physical decline.

She ends her treatise by assuring him of her love for him, and that she, who is his spiritual mother 'through your baptism and in affection' prays that he will be a true *'Miles Christi'*, a true soldier of Christ. In writing this treatise for her nephew, Elisabeth was consciously thinking that it would be circulated among other young men, perhaps through her work among young people and their families, that all young men would be strong in their faith and all would be 'soldiers of Christ'.

Notes

[1] E. Leseur, *Light in the Darkness* (Manchester USA: Sophia Institute Press, 1998), p. 84.
[2] *Ibid.*, p. 91.
[3] *Ibid.*
[4] *Ibid.*, p. 92.
[5] *Ibid.*
[6] *Ibid.*, p. 101.
[7] *Ibid.*, p. 102.
[8] *Ibid., p. 100.*

[9] *Ibid.*, p. 132.
[10] *Ibid.*, p. 133.
[11] J. K. Ruffing RSM (edited, translated and introduced by), *Elisabeth Leseur* (New York: Classics of Western Spirituality, Paulist Press, 2005), p. 189.

8

APOSTOLATE OF PRAYER

IN March 1906 Elisabeth went with Félix to Vienna on business, the last time they went abroad on any extended trip. On 6 August 1906 she came to the end of her notebook and to the end of her diary, at least for the time being. In it, she had not kept a day-to-day account but, as she wrote, an account of 'the stages of my life and my soul'. She had kept the diary for seven years, and through its pages she could see how Providence had guided her steps, even when she was unaware of it, and which she came to understand only later. As she meditated on how God had guided her over the years she saw herself as God's 'privileged child'; she had been given great graces, and because of that she knew that 'casting my eyes over the past and looking forward toward the future with serenity, this future can no longer bring any true sorrow, because God is my horizon everywhere'.[1]

She realised that the pain and suffering of the past two years, and especially the death of Juliette, had refined and purified her and brought her closer to God. New horizons were now opening out to her, and she wanted to be 'another woman, a Christian, an apostle'. She knew that her health would not improve, but she could accept this with serenity. Facing these new horizons demanded ever closer co-operation with the graces of God, so she made several resolutions.

The first was *silence*. She had been aware that with her health problems and her grief over Juliette's death, she had spoken of her inner trials more freely than she had normally done. Also, that she had also revealed more of her inner life than she had wanted. Now, she felt she should reveal less of herself, unless it would be of benefit to others. She would go to Mass, receive the sacraments, have her times of prayer and devotions as unobtrusively as possible, firstly, so that there would be no hint of pride, 'that I remain humble', but also because she did not want to 'provoke a spirit of obstinacy and ignorance with which I am surrounded'.[2] Despite Félix's softening of attitude toward the practice of her faith, it was still a closed book to him, provoking his scorn.

She was determined to continue her charitable work, but she also wanted to be stricter with herself, with her use of her time, the way she conducted herself towards others, and the inner discipline of doing and being everything before God and with God. Without that discipline, all the demands on her time would make her life chaotic—running her household, performing her charitable works and the unexpected calls on her time, her care and concern for her extended family, as well as carrying out the social functions and obligations of her state in life:

> To sum up: To *reserve* for God alone the depths of my soul and my interior life as a Christian. To *give* to others serenity, charm, kindness, useful words and deeds. To make Christian truth loved through me, but to speak of it only at an explicit demand or a need so clear as to seem truly providential. To preach by prayer, sacrifice and example. To be *austere* to myself, and as *attractive* as possible to others.[3]

However, in closing her diary, she opened another notebook two months later to record her 'Resolutions' in the way she would carry out this apostolate. She recognised that she could not be too rigid, because circumstances would change day by day in the organisation of her life. Always, she would put Félix at the centre. This was not through the somewhat erroneous concept of servile submission to her husband that some derive from St Paul's words about women being obedient to their husband, but far more on the second precept, so often omitted, that husbands should love their wives, in a way that mirrored Christ's self-giving love for His Church. There was such a strong marriage in the Leseur household because there was this mutual self-giving, with both loving each other deeply. Elisabeth writes beautiful words in her new notebook, which reveals the tender and delicate love she had for her husband:

> *First my duty to my dear husband*: tenderness that has not even the merit of duty, constant care to be useful and gracious to him. Above all, to be extremely reserved concerning matters of faith, which are still veiled to him. If a quiet statement should sometimes be necessary, or if I can fruitfully show him a little of what is in my heart, that must at least be an event, done after careful thought, performed in all gentleness and sincerity.
>
> Let him see the fruit but not the sap, my life but not the faith that transforms it, the light that is in me but not a word of Him who brings it to my soul; let him see God without hearing His name. Only on those lines, I think, must I hope for the conversion of and sanctity of the dear companion of my life, my beloved Félix.[4]

She did not reveal in this passage the cost to of this herself, the loneliness and isolation she felt in the midst of a happy marriage; the sorrow that she could not share with the one she loved so dearly what meant most to her in her life, her union with God.

As the year turned into 1907, she recorded the progress of her ever-deepening life of prayer, of maintaining that serenity and sweetness which was so characteristic of her. However, her health was beginning to deteriorate, and she was often confined to her bed with a fever and the pain of her condition, the hepatitis and a chronic internal abscess.

It was not possible to hide her illness from her mother, and to her, of course, it was just another heartbreak to bear so soon after Juliette's death. During their usual stay in Jougne, high in the Alps, her mother could see her discomfort, although the good air did help somewhat. Elisabeth herself was totally given to the will of God but could see it was much more difficult for her mother, to whom she was so close. She and Félix had to return to Paris three weeks earlier than the rest of the family, and before she left Elisabeth wrote a long letter to her mother to help her come to terms with her daughter's illness. In it, Elisabeth said she wanted to 'transform your pain, calm your mind, and give you a supernatural aim to all that is so naturally good in you'.[5] Her mother was a devout Catholic, she said her prayers, attended Mass, but it did not bring her that interior calm and awareness of the presence of God that was so dominant in her daughter. Perhaps, as some lay Catholics thought at the time, she felt that meditation, contemplation, was just for contemplative monks and nuns and not for her, and was even somewhat fearful of it as some exotic exercise.

From the letter it seems that Elisabeth had broached the subject of meditation to her, but 'your nature shrinks from the thought of contemplation, and that you are alarmed by the very word *meditation,* just as the idea of entering a church would frighten an unbeliever'. Her mother, though, would undoubtedly tell the unbeliever how delightful it really is to be in the presence of One whom he does not know. 'I can tell you the same thing about meditation; the name repels you, but the thing itself

Apostolate of Prayer

is very beautiful and profound, being the foundation of the Christian life.'

Elisabeth then goes on to help her mother into the practice of meditation, which is a classic of spiritual guidance. She advised her mother to begin gently, spending perhaps only a few moments a day, but to persevere even when she is disinclined. In addition, she should seek the will of God in everything, to put God first. The result and the fruit will be joy, 'an interior happiness, proceeding from God Himself'. This happiness is not diminished by trials and sufferings, but even enhanced, if they are accepted, because they bring us 'close to the Eternal'.

In this letter Elisabeth gives a precious insight into her own inner life and how she herself was coping with her illness. She hoped it would give her mother peace of mind and the serenity of soul she saw in her daughter. For Elisabeth, the practice of meditation, contemplation, had reached a very deep level, which she describes as 'the gathering of oneself into the very depths of one's being, to that point where, as theologians tell us, in the silencing of outward things, God is found'.[6] It was what made sense of her life.

Félix, too, was beginning to observe his wife and the way her prayer life was developing and strengthening her in her daily life. In Paris, she called this a 'scattered' life. With the proviso that family obligations would take precedence she devised a framework of daily prayer and meditation, Mass and Communion three times a week, regular Confession and a monthly 'retreat' day in which she tried to spend more time in prayer and spiritual reading, especially following the Church's liturgical year. She explained in her 'Resolutions' what this following of the liturgical year meant for her:

> Catholic liturgy has great charm for me; I love to live, in the course of the year, the great collective

life of the Church, uniting myself with its joys and sorrows, joining my feeble prayers with its prayers, my weak voice with its powerful voice.[7]

In the liturgy she would follow Christ's life from his Incarnation to his triumphant return, and she also felt united to the saints throughout the ages who had followed him, and whose birthdays into the life of heaven were celebrated year by year. She knew herself to be also a 'living cell in the great Catholic union'.

Family came first, especially her love and devotion to her husband, but Félix recalled an occasion when he had interrupted her prayer time over some trivial matter.

'Oh, I was praying,' Elizabeth told him, 'please, in your kindness, don't disturb me again during these times that I have set aside for prayer. If you only knew how vital this time is for me'. Félix was very struck by this and never disturbed her time of prayer unnecessarily again.

Félix, of course, was out most of the time at work when in Paris and so did not know the full extent of his wife's prayer life. But at Jougne he was able to observe her more closely. There, Elisabeth was able to follow a much more structured regime. At about 10 o'clock in the morning she would go to her room for an hour of prayer. The children knew that she wasn't to be disturbed during this time, calling it 'Aunt Bébeth's meditation'. Later she would join the group of family and friends on the terrace, relaxing on her chaise longue, and even when she was writing her letters was still cheerfully joining in the conversation.

During the day she would make several visits to the little chapel in the village. She was there one day when a young woman and her mother came in and saw Elizabeth absorbed in prayer. They stayed for a little while, but so great an impression did she make on them that the mother said, 'Let us go now, we aren't worthy to be near her'.

Elizabeth herself would have been extremely embarrassed about this, if she had known about it, because she was deeply humble and never displayed her prayerfulness, doing her best to hide the depth of her prayer from others. The paradox was that her life now was so imbued with prayer that it emanated from her in everything she did, even without her realising it.

Elisabeth never saw her prayer as distinct from her care for others, distinct from everything she did during the day, and she also knew that it had to be backed up by self-denial. Her daily life, of course, as a lay person gave her many opportunities for this—joining in the often shallow talk of her social class, and the need to dress in the manner expected of her position in society, while keeping it as simple as she could. There were the times of sitting in silence when her faith was attacked and ridiculed, the isolation of spirit of being unable to share that faith. Even with the self-denial and suffering her illness imposed on her she tried to mortify herself beyond this. Félix admitted that he was quite a gourmet, enjoying good food and fine wines. He noticed that Elisabeth would sometimes decline a dish and make the excuse that it was because of her health. He would think no more of it and didn't insist. It was just one example of the simple and unobtrusive way she mortified herself.

Like all the Arrighi family, Elisabeth disliked milk and milk products, but she had a special aversion to the skin on warmed milk. Félix bought her an elegant little strainer so that she could strain her drinks but later on he realised she was not using it. When he asked her why, she replied that it was silly to allow such a small thing to overcome her.

Back in Paris, she had been helped somewhat by her holiday in Jougne but by October her illness could no longer be ignored or hidden behind the veil of graciousness. Dr Duran, her brother-in-law, was also her regular doctor, and Félix thought highly of him. They had studied medicine together and had become great friends, which is how Elisabeth's sister, Amélie, had met him; Félix also had a high regard for his medical skills. Now he was joined by another doctor, M Létienne, to see whether she might have to have an operation. They decided that a surgeon, Professor Gosset, who, although he was still young, from the same generation as Félix and Duran, was the most qualified to perform the operation. The consultation took place 19 October, and Elisabeth wrote to her mother on the 29th, to tell of her the outcome.

She said that the three doctors were unanimous in their decision: the operation was so dangerous and serious that they were unwilling to agree on it. Instead, they recommended rest and immobility. The fact that all three agreed on this gave Elisabeth peace of mind. As a result, though, Elisabeth was forced to give up much of her charitable work, returning to it as her health permitted. When she had to give up active work with the charities she acted as secretary for them instead. She longed to be an apostle, but as active work gradually became beyond her she saw this as the beginning of a new life for her, 'imposed on me by the divine Will—a sedentary life, which resembles a sort of spiritual retreat offered to my soul by Providence at a time when my years enter into maturity'.[8]

She saw herself as having an even more fruitful apostolate, that of prayer. The apostolate of prayer, as she saw it, and which was the well-spring of her spirituality, was powerful precisely because it was not bound by time or space, embedded, as it was, in the Communion of Saints. It was doubly powerful, too, when linked to suffering, because suffering could be made fruitful for souls when united to the suffering of Christ on the Cross:

> To ask God to draw on the inner reserve of suffering that I bear within the depths of my soul, in favour of souls and of those I love. Always to welcome trials, little or big, to accept them and to offer them. Then, to keep silence and continue to act in all gentleness and sincerity.[9]

The doctrine of the fruitfulness of suffering united to the suffering of Christ is deeply embedded in Catholic spirituality; this was not suffering sought for its own sake as it had sometimes tended to be, and Catholic religious orders had and always were, in the forefront of alleviating suffering and illness. Elisabeth gave it a slant that befitted her status as a lay person. For her, austerity meant hiding her sufferings, whether of body or soul, behind her 'veil' of silence and graciousness towards others. It did not mean denying herself the remedies that could keep her as healthy and active as possible:

> *Personal austerity.* By austerity I do not mean, of course, anything harmful to the body or to health. I must, on the contrary, watch out for and try to improve my health, since it may be an instrument in the service of God and of souls. But in this illness with which I am afflicted, the precautions I am obliged to take, the discomfort it brings, and the privations it sometimes imposes on me (or at least may in future impose on me), there is a plentiful source of mortification. Apart from that there are numerous opportunities for self-sacrifice, without anyone knowing of it or suffering because of it; on the contrary, our personal immolation will often be of actual benefit to others. To perform these mortifications and sacrifices in a spirit of penance, of *reparation* to God and to the Heart of Jesus, and to obtain the salvation of sinners.[10]

Following her doctors' advice she now spent most of her time at home and took advantage of her relative immobility to increase her prayer and meditation, to a point where it became mystical. Elisabeth had a full set of the works of Saint Teresa of Avila, and during this period read and pondered deeply on her writings. Teresa was one of her favourite saints, Elisabeth liking her because of her gaiety, her vigorous love of life, which suited her own personality well. Visitors were for a time limited to family and close friends, and she never lost her gaiety and charm during their visits. Perhaps only Félix knew how remarkable this was, because, having trained as a doctor, he knew that Elisabeth's condition was one that usually made patients irritable and bad tempered.

She had a further relapse in June, and it was decided that she would benefit from the clearer air in Jougne. Félix knew a high official in the rail company and arranged to have special provision made for her. She was taken by car to the station and a special carriage was added for her, with a bed in it; the train was allowed stop at the Hospital, the last stop before it entered Switzerland, to shorten the journey to Jougne.

They stayed there until October, and by that time Elisabeth was recovered enough for them to go to Ouchy, by Lake Geneva, rather than returning straight home to Paris. It provided a transition from the mountain air of Jougne to the less salubrious air of Paris. As always, they were sad at leaving, but before setting off they visited the little church, Elisabeth to pray, Félix to view a tapestry altar cloth that Elisabeth had made for the altar in the lady chapel.

In Ouchy they spent most of their time outdoors, most often beside the lake, where a gentle breeze refreshed the convalescent. Elisabeth loved the scenery, which expanded her spirit: her doctors had previously remarked on her strong constitution, despite her illness, and it was undoubtedly her positive attitude, borne of her strong faith, that contributed to this. She spoke of her delight in her surroundings in a letter to her mother 19 October:

> Yesterday we were again treated to a splendid lake, with its vast horizons, and in a boat we had a beautiful view of the sun setting....
>
> The weather is warm and delicious by the lake, better even than at Jougne. On Friday, we took a trip in a boat for four hours, as far as Villeneuve. Saturday, leaving at 10 o'clock, we dined aboard the boat, stopping for an hour in Geneva, and returning at 5.15. Sunday, a tour of the bottom end of the lake, and then leaving for Paris at 11 o'clock in the evening. In the morning I went to Mass; Félix, with great goodness, found a little chapel very near the hotel, intimate and with a very prayerful atmosphere, founded and maintained by the Princess of Sayn-Wittgenstein. I attended the 8 o'clock Mass and received communion with quite a few other people, in great joy and thanksgiving to the good God.[11]

Sadly, when they returned to Paris her health swiftly deteriorated again, and she was bedridden for a few months as the year turned into 1908. In her notebook she speaks of illness and physical exhaustion and of the boredom and monotony of being ill. Félix knew that her illness gave rise to irritability, but perhaps he was not fully aware of the efforts Elisabeth made not to give in to it. She herself probably did not realise that this was a side effect of her illness, and could therefore be quite hard on herself:

> One must do everything with even greater calm and purpose, and guard oneself from exterior agitation by an even greater recollectedness. Not

> to allow myself the slightest movement of impatience, and to fight unceasingly against every inner temptation to irritability. To punish and humble myself for it afterward.[12]

To be unable to go to Mass during this period was the greatest deprivation for her, although it seems that towards the end Holy Communion was brought to her. However, by April the worst was over, and she could look back and see that despite, or perhaps because of, this period of testing, the Lord had done great things in her:

> The apparent inertia, the inner destitution, the humiliating prostration of body and mind were all covering and hiding a mysterious work of grace that was taking place in the depths of my soul. And now I state with joy that God has made me take a great step forward in the way of renunciation and self-denial, teaching me even to do without His sweet consolations.[13]

Just before she left Jougne during their stay there the following year, she went to the little chapel, and on 2 October renewed her baptismal vows and made a new consecration of herself, which completed the 'innermost consecration begun at the tomb of the Apostles, starting a new era in my spiritual life, and binding me irrevocably to the way of the evangelical counsels, the only one in which my soul can breathe now'.[14]

It was clear to her now that 'the Divine Will does not intend me for action'. Prayer was to be her apostolate, prayer, 'the all-powerful force that, coming through the Heart of Jesus right into the very bosom of God, seizes, attracts, and in some way plunges grace into souls'.[15] Always, though, she allied it to suffering and the practice of charity which to her were equally powerful forms of prayer. Suffering would always be with her now, she accepted, and even from her sickbed she could give her charity away in whatever form she could. This could be through the cheerfulness she showed to her many visitors, in the letters she wrote, and any forms of activity that were within her scope.

In May of 1910 she had another worry, with the severe illness of her sister Amélie, so Elisabeth made a pilgrimage to Lourdes to pray for her recovery. On her birthday in October she wrote that her watchword for the coming winter, with its round of social functions and her continuing charity work would be 'resolution'. She wanted to purify her intentions, that all she did would be for God; 'that is what will sustain the spirit of prayer in my soul and make it shine in my life'.[16] As always, she wanted to cloak her inner life, 'forgetfulness of self concealed by smiles'. As always, she recognised that 'the combat of intellects will never open the way to God, but a ray of charity sometimes illumines the path'.

She would not be drawn into discussion of religious matters, and how wise this was she revealed in an entry in her 'Resolutions' describing:

> Bitter suffering of an evening spent in hearing my faith and spiritual things mocked at, attacked, and criticised. God helped me to maintain interior charity and exterior calm; to deny or betray nothing, and yet not to irritate by too rigid assertions. But how much effort and inner distress this involves, and how necessary is divine grace to assist my weakness![17]

This restraint and calm was all the more remarkable, given the fact that she was struggling with her pain and ill health and inner fatigue, as well as the isolation she felt. But soon God would answer her prayers for what she had longed for, for so many years, a 'soul-mate', one who shared the depth of her faith, and to whom she could open herself with complete confidence.

Notes

1. E. Leseur, *My Spirit Rejoices* (Manchester: New Hampshire: Sophia Institute Press, 1996), p. 108.
2. *Ibid.*, p. 109.
3. *Ibid.*, p. 110.
4. *Ibid.*, p. 116.
5. E. Leseur, *Light in the Darkness* (Manchester, New Hampshire: Sophia Institute Press, 1998), p. 35.
6. J. K. Ruffing RSM (edited, translated and introduced by), *Elisabeth Leseur* (New York: Classics of Western Spirituality, Paulist Press, 2005), p. 204.
7. E. Leseur, *My Spirit Rejoices*, p. 145.
8. *Ibid.*, p. 128.
9. *Ibid.*, p. 122.
10. *Ibid.*, p. 118.
11. R. P. M.-A. Leseur (Félix Leseur), *Vie d'Elisabeth Leseur* (Paris: J. de Gigord, Editeur, 1946), pp. 189ff.
12. E. Leseur, *My Spirit Rejoices*, p. 133.
13. *Ibid.*, p. 134.
14. *Ibid.*, p. 135.
15. *Ibid.*, p. 136.
16. *Ibid.*, p. 132.
17. *Ibid.*, p. 148.

9

A SOUL SISTER

On 10 July, a friend drove Félix and Elisabeth from Paris to Jougne for a short break. On the way, they stopped off for lunch at Beaune and decided to visit the famous Hôtel-Dieu there. This hospital for the terminally ill was already famous for its beautiful paintings and stunning architecture. It was founded in 1443 by Nicolas Rolin, chancellor of Burgundy, as a hospital for the poor, and is one of the finest examples of French fifteenth-century architecture. It already housed an impressive museum that attracted many visitors. At its centre was the great hall with painted ceilings, which the bedridden could see from their beds, and next to it was the chapel, which was so arranged that the sick could attend Mass from their beds. It was rightly called 'the Palace of the Poor'. Everything was done so that they would take pride of place and be surrounded by beauty. Coming out of one of the side rooms Elisabeth saw a little invalid of eight years old in the courtyard under one of the balconies and stopped to speak to her for a while. Her name was Marie Ballard, and she was terminally ill with tuberculosis. She came from a very poor family whose father was also ill with the same disease. Elisabeth asked her if there was anything she would like, and Marie said that she would love some postcards; Elisabeth promised she would send her some.

After they left, Marie was excited when, a little later, she told the sister looking after her about the beautiful lady who had promised to send her postcards. The sister, Marie Goby, was somewhat sceptical of the promise, because she knew only too well that visitors would make promises but forget them when they went on their way. She warned Marie not to get her hopes up, but Elisabeth was not like others. She bought a postcard of Besançon that same evening and followed it up with more on the following days.

Sister Goby wrote a little note of thanks on Marie's behalf, but included a letter of her own that expressed the delight the cards had given to the little girl:

> Madame,
>
> I do not have the honour of knowing you, and yet allow me to join my respectful thanks to those of my dear little invalid. I was profoundly touched by your delicate charity towards that poor little child. Your lovely cards are for her a ray of sunshine; I assure you that on receiving them, I saw a smile dawn on her young face which usually bore the imprint of sadness and suffering, and I myself was happy and ask God to repay such delicate goodness.[1]

The Leseurs returned to Paris at the end of July, and Elisabeth wrote to Sister Goby to ask if there was anything else that Marie would really like. The sister wrote back that cake and fruit were no longer suitable for the invalid, but when she had asked Marie herself what she would like, the little girl, who had had so little in her short life, asked for a doll that she could dress and undress. Elisabeth lost no time in sending her one. When it arrived, Marie was ecstatic with the doll that exceeded her expectations; she had never seen such a beautiful one. Each morning was a new blessing for her, wrote Sr. Goby, as well as all the other good things Elisabeth was now sending them for all the other patients, too:

> As for me, it is I who must thank you. Thanks to you, I will have the sweet satisfaction of giving pleasure to these poor little sad and suffering ones.

> It is for me so good to be able to give such treats to these dear children I love so much! .... I have never known such sweet joy. So from the bottom of my heart I thank you.[2]

Sister Goby told Elisabeth that Marie had never received any instruction in the Faith; she did not even know how to make the sign of the cross and was being given instruction so that she could make her First Communion before she died. Elisabeth therefore sent her little books that would help her.

This was a busy and also worrying time for the Leseurs, which made Elisabeth's thoughtful kindness to Marie all the more telling. In November they moved from their apartment in the rue d'Argenson, which had been their home for twelve years, to 16, rue de Marignan, on the Champs Elysée, which would be their final home together. They also heard from the Duvents that their eldest son, Michel, not quite sixteen years old, had died from tuberculosis 22 September. The two families were very close, and Elisabeth, who dearly loved the charming and gifted young man, was heartbroken at his death. She immediately went to Neuilly to be with the family, and Félix joined her a few days later. She later wrote to Aline Duvent:

> I am happy that you feel immersed in an atmosphere of sympathy, and also of faith, for it is this faith which your poor, sad heart needs, and, according to the words of Saint Augustine, 'it will be restless until it rests in God'. You desire it, and if you ask for it with confidence and perseverance, by your prayers and your seeking, it will be given to you, for Providence will never deprive itself of those appeals of a soul.[3]

Elisabeth was also worried about an additional problem with her health. For a while, she had noticed a small tumour on her breast, which had also concerned her brother-in-law. To try and rectify it, her doctors required her to wear a painfully tight apparatus about her chest, hoping that this would avoid the need for surgery. It was yet one more burden and discomfort for her to carry, which she struggled with at first, but soon she was accepting it as another cross given her to bear with a smile in her heart; a 'hair shirt' that would substitute for the one she would never be allowed to wear.

It was an additional sorrow for her, then, when on 17 December Sr Goby wrote to Elisabeth to tell her the sad news that Marie had died, but not before she had made her First Communion. Elisabeth responded by sending her a copy of the account she had written about her sister Juliette, and it was only then that Sr Goby told her that Marie had called her doll Juliette, with neither of them realising that it was the name of Elisabeth's sister.

By then, the correspondence between the two of them had become much less formal, and it seemed as if it was Juliette herself, from heaven, who was bringing the two of them together in a true soul-friendship.

They were beginning to share news of their respective families; Elisabeth gave Sr Goby news of her breast cancer concerns, and to ask for her prayer. As for Elisabeth, she met the possibility of breast cancer with the serenity expressed in a letter to her mother: 'I have a principle that when a good comes to me without my seeking it, then it is the will of the good God for me'.[4]

On the last day of the year 1910 she looked back on it as a year the chief characteristic of which had been privation, but she did not leave it at that. Through all the sadness, aridity and suffering, she recognised that 'the Blessed Master has taught me a stronger, deeper love, stripped of conscious happiness; and it is from the bottom of my heart that I offer Him the year that is gone and the one that is to come'.[5] Knowing that the coming year would mean facing perhaps incurable breast cancer, she offered it to the Lord with all her heart and soul:

> O Lord, I abandon myself to You and wish to love You still more. Give health and holiness to those I love, salvation and all Your graces to souls, and peace and expansion to Your Church.
>
> For myself, I ask one thing: let me love You, without joy or comfort if need be, and to use me for the spreading of Your spiritual Kingdom in souls, Jesus my Saviour.[6]

Above all, she offered whatever would be for the conversion of the one she loved best in the world, her husband Félix. It was with this serenity that she attended the clinic of the surgeon Dr Reclus, 7 April 1911, who agreed to operate on her two days later. Unfortunately, Félix was unable to be with her for that visit, as he was preparing for an immanent annual general meeting of the Conservateurs, the insurance company for which he worked.

The evening before she was admitted to the clinic on the rue de la Pompe the Leseurs dined with the Le Dantecs, and everyone was profoundly impressed with Elisabeth's serenity. The explanation for this was found in the 'pact' she had made with God on the Feast of St Joseph 17 March:

> Special prayer. An intimate compact between my soul and God, my heart and the heart of Jesus, through the intercession of the Blessed Virgin and under the protection of St Joseph and St Teresa. Confidence this time of being heard again. Now, O Lord, I await the fulfilment of Your blessed promises, and I wish to receive faithfully what they bring me in Your name.
>
> May God be blessed![7]

She entered the clinic the following day, which was Palm Sunday. The clinic had previously been a Carmelite monastery, from which the friars had been expelled following the 1902 Law of Associations. However, the clinic had direct access to the chapel, so that the patients could follow the Mass and other services, without having to go outside, something that was of great consolation to Elisabeth. She attended Mass before her operation, which took place the following day at 9.30 in the morning. Félix was staying in a room next to hers in the clinic, and as Elisabeth was being prepared for the operation he was far more anxious than she was, although she tried to hide any anxiety she had. The operation was a success, and the days following it were a time of great blessing for them both.

They grew in ever greater intimacy with each other at this time, as he supported her through the inevitable pain of recovery, but their surroundings helped. Even Félix found himself soothed by the calm atmosphere of the old monastery and its interior garden, far from external concerns. For them both it was a time of great sweetness and they left the clinic with regret but with gratitude for that lovely time of intimacy together, to return to their apartment.

The evening following their return, Félix found on his desk a note from Elisabeth that was a testimony to her exquisite tenderness:

> It is you, my dear Félix, who will have the first lines written by me after that operation. I would like them to be able to express my profound tenderness and this gratitude, the sweetest burden of which has yet increased during those days of trial; my patron, St Elizabeth, changed humble bread into roses; you found ways of transforming into joys and consolations the most intimate and very profound sufferings. In my helplessness where I loved you even more; where I pay you my debt of gratitude,

I confide to God that dear belief. Better than I can, he will repay you a hundredfold for what you have given to me and what you have done for me—my beloved, I embrace you with all my tenderness.

Your wife

Elisabeth[8]

If the year 1910 had been a difficult one for Elisabeth, this year would bring her incomparable blessings. She still had weeks of chemotherapy to undergo, but in June she received a letter from Sr Goby suggesting that, since it was almost a year since the Leseurs had visited Beaune, 'seeing the number of strangers who arrive all the time, I often ask myself if there would not be the joy, one day, of meeting you, and I allow myself, with the eye of an inquisitor [surveying the visitors], always hoping to meet you'.[9]

This letter would have given Elisabeth great joy, written on the Feast of Pentecost, which was the special Feast day of the Hôtel-Dieu. Sr Goby echoed Elisabeth's own hopes that they could meet, adding, 'My vow, which is my prayer, is that during the length of years we are able more and more and better and better to live for Our Lord, for his interests, for his work and also for the our dear one [Félix] and for those for whom you have so great an affection!'[10]

Elisabeth replied that Félix could not leave Paris until the end of July, and she herself had to finish her course of chemotherapy. They would then be staying for a short while with her brother's family in Bourgogne during the first half of August. Sr Goby herself would be going with her mother on their usual pilgrimage to Ars, but that would not be until after the Feast of the Assumption, 15 August. A date therefore was fixed for 12 August, when the Leseur's would be making their journey to Jougne.

When they left Peter's family, they brought their niece Marie with them. They stayed in Chagny, and Marie, who was very tired after the journey, slept until 8 o'clock, then at 9 o'clock she and Félix dined together while Elisabeth went to the Hôtel-Dieu for Mass in the charming chapel with the Sisters; among them was Sr Goby, although Elisabeth did not yet know which one she was. Elisabeth loved the sight of the nuns in their white habits and headdresses, which were based on a local headdress, not the usual veil.

After the thanksgiving, one of the sisters came up to her and introduced herself; Sr Goby had had no difficulty in knowing, from her demeanour, who Elisabeth was among the other visitors. They went to a small room to have breakfast, then after a time of talking together they assisted at the Solemn Mass for the whole hospital. Sr Goby then had to leave her a while, so Elisabeth spent a quiet time in the lovely, calm garden until the sister joined her once more. They had a long time together, with Elisabeth sharing more of her inner self than she had ever been able to before.

On the surface, it seemed an unlikely friendship, between the sophisticated and well-educated woman whose vocation was to be in the world, and the nun who had devoted her life to caring for the sick and dying. Sister Marie Goby was at this time 46 years old, one year older than Elisabeth, and had been a nursing sister for 23 years. Elisabeth's spirituality was built around the Mass, Confession, following the liturgical year, intense reading of the Scriptures and spiritual classics. Apart from her love of the Sacred Heart, she did not feel drawn to 'devotions'.

In Sr Goby's congregation their obligations of course centred round the Mass, and they recited the Little Office of Our Lady and the Office for the Dead daily. Apart from that the sisters were free to follow their own spiritual tastes, and Sr Goby was drawn to the devotions that were not to Elisabeth's liking. However, the nun had an equally cultured background, and both found themselves, following their different paths, aiming for the same goal and the same depth of union with God. They were also both united in their love for the poor and the sick, Elisabeth by her work for the various charities and Sr Goby with her vocation to nursing the sick in the Hôtel Dieu and her deep love for those she nursed.

There was an immediate meeting of minds and hearts and in both a sense of meeting a friend. Both enjoyed the writings of Madame Swetchine (1782–1857), a Russian-French convert to the Church, who had organized a famous Parisian salon and was noted for her works on mysticism. A few days after this meeting Sr Goby quoted from her in a letter to express what she felt about it, writing 'There are some people one has never seen before but one recognises them the first time one sees them! On seeing you, dear Madame, I knew that what Mme. Swetchine had said was true!'[11]

That same letter gives an insight into the effect Elisabeth had on people. Sr Goby had come to know Elisabeth's soul in her letters and in the little booklet she had written about Juliette:

> I had seen the radiance of that same spirit on your face when I saw you near the tabernacle of our little chapel when I approached you for the first time!
>
> I found it again shining through the features of your face and expressing itself in our conversation in our intimate hour in the morning! And then, oh! instantly I loved you and felt so attracted to you! Yes, I want my soul to become a true Sister to yours.[12]

A month later she told Elisabeth what their friendship meant for her also, in having a spiritual guide in her life:

> Have I told you that for thirty years, I have dreamed of a friend whose soul would be a true Sister to mine? And I feel that the Good Master has just given it to me, and would you not want what I want and guard it ardently?[13]

In the meantime, on that first day of meeting, Elisabeth returned to their hotel for lunch, then all three returned to the hospital. Félix, as well as Marie, immediately took to Sr Goby; they had a common interest with Félix's medical background, but he was also taken with her charm, her culture, her sweetness. After Vespers, which even Félix attended, Sr Goby took them on a tour of the hospital and Félix was especially struck by the sight of the nuns and the simple beauty of the Vespers chant. He could appreciate the aesthetics even if he could not understand the inner meaning of it.

It was with great emotion that they made their farewells, and for Elisabeth it was a day of great blessing, but one which would be of vital import in the years ahead. In a delightful phrase, she said that the encounter with one who would henceforth be her soul sister brought 'a smile of happiness' to her.

Notes

[1] E. Leseur, *Lettres Sur La Souffrance* (Paris: Les Éditions du Cerf, 2012), p. 41.
[2] *Ibid.*, p. 43.
[3] R. P. M.-A. Leseur (Félix Leseur), *Vie d'Elisabeth Leseur* (Paris: J. de Gigord, Editeur, 1946), p. 326.
[4] *Ibid.*, p. 194.
[5] E. Leseur, *My Spirit Rejoices* (Manchester, New Hampshire: Sophia Institute Press, 1996), p. 150.
[6] *Ibid.*, p. 151.
[7] *Ibid.*, p. 157.

[8] M.-A. Leseur, *Vie*, pp. 198ff.
[9] E. Leseur, *Lettres Sur La Souffrance*, p. 57.
[10] *Ibid.*, p. 56.
[11] *Ibid.*, p. 64.
[12] J. K. Ruffing RSM (edited, translated and introduced by), *Elisabeth Leseur* (New York: Paulist Press, Classics of Western Spirituality, 2005), p. 170.
[13] *Ibid.*, p. 65.

10

SUFFERING ACCEPTED AND OFFERED

Sr Goby's mother lived in a village nearby, and it was their custom to spend a few days every year going on pilgrimage together. They had intended to set off for Ars, the parish of the saintly Curé of Ars, St Jean Vianney, the day after the Leseur's visit, but had to postpone it because Sr Goby contracted a stomach bug. They therefore left towards the end of August, from where Sr Goby sent a letter to Elisabeth, with some souvenirs from Ars. Already, their letters to each other reflected the deeper intimacy between them; for Elisabeth, Sr Goby was 'my very dear Sister', Elisabeth was 'my very dear friend'. Meanwhile, from Beaune, Elisabeth's party continued on their journey to Jougne. Marie had to return home at the end of the month, but others of their family joined them a little later. There, where Elisabeth was happiest, surrounded by family, she found healing for soul and body in the beauty of her surroundings. Félix, too, was able to relax and enjoy the peace and the good air.

It also gave Elisabeth time to write to Sr Goby. With her usual generosity she asked if there was anything she could send that would give pleasure to the patients. She was reading Fr Faber, the famous English convert, and offered to send her a copy of the book on their return to Paris, knowing that Sr Goby also enjoyed his work.

She was also able to write about the intimacies of her inner life that she could reveal in such depth to no others. For her part, Sr Goby shared with Elisabeth that the dream of her religious life, the only thing she asked of Jesus was to love him and serve him only, working only in his service. In reply, Elisabeth wrote that she had unhappily to curtail her charitable works because of her ill health, but recognised that her sufferings, accepted and offered, however feebly, was her apostolate now. Knowing that she had a confidant to whom she could tell everything, she admitted that the suffering of heart and spirit were greater than her physical trials, but this, too, she offered at the foot of the Cross.

Elisabeth said that her health was as well as possible, but that it could change at any moment. 'I abandon myself to Providence and live above all in the present moment'.[1] This proved to be true. Félix and Elisabeth made a three-day trip to Lake Geneva, where his brother and sister-in-law were, then travelled to Lake Thoune before all of them returned to Jougne on the Oberland train. The day after their return, 22 September, Elisabeth became seriously ill with an infected lymph gland of her right arm and with a high temperature, a consequence of her operation in April. She was confined to her bed for over a fortnight and made the long journey back to Paris by car, in easy stages.

Her doctors forbade her to write during this time, so it was not until 6 October that Félix allowed her to take up her pen again and write to Sr Goby. However much pain she had, 'despite privations, suffering, sadness, the profound joy remains in the depths of my soul, and I give heartfelt thanks to God, striving to give everything to him with a smile'.[2] She had reached a stage where the joy of her union with God could not be disturbed by whatever pain, interior or exterior, she was experiencing.

On 19 October 1911, three days after her 45th birthday, she decided to write a diary again, while still keeping a separate notebook for her 'Resolutions'. She began the diary by looking back on her life, seeing God's hand in 'the wonderful work of inner conversion', the slow, silent action of Providence at work even when she was not aware of it, or even indifferent to it those many years ago. She could look back with profound gratitude and with a song of joy for her present life, made up of both joys and sorrows:

> May my grief and supernatural joy, my whole life and even my death proclaim the greatness of divine love, the holiness of the Church, the tenderness and sweetness of the Heart of Jesus, the existence and the beauty of the supernatural life, and the reality of our Christian hopes.[3]

Recovered somewhat, she took up again their social life, which was now so wearisome to her: 'I occupy myself with clothes and furs ... and talk about them, so as to give no hint of austerities'.[4] 'I try to keep my resolution of outward "worldliness". When my soul longs for recollectedness and prayer, when I want to act, but act by deeds, for God and my neighbour'.[5]

To Sr Goby she wrote:

> Let us learn to smile at all that he sends: joy or sorrow, illness, consolations or heavy dryness of spirit, even these meannesses and—this is for me—these little social obligations and all external things that weigh heavily on a soul that longs more and more to be with God. There is in the depths of me an ardent desire for withdrawal, of a hidden, silent life that the world and even some Christians do not understand.[6]

The New Year of 1912 brought fresh anxieties with the continuing illness of her sister Amélie; in March her mother was also ill with chronic bronchitis, on top of the arthritis that was making life more and more difficult for her. Then in May, her nephew Maurice was playing with a toy cap gun which exploded, causing such injury to his right hand that at one point it was feared it might have to be amputated. Happily, this did not happen. Elisabeth was so grateful for this that in June she wanted to go to Lourdes to give thanks for his recovery, also to pray for her sister. As well as Amélie and Maurice, Félix came with them because he would not leave Elisabeth in her precarious state of health. His mother was delighted that he was going on the pilgrimage, hoping that it might lead to his conversion; she asked him to pray for her at the Grotto, to Félix's amusement. He replied to her:

> A few words in haste, as we are just on the point of leaving, because you are relying on me. I will carry the prayer with me that you ask me for. But, you understand, what must be must be. The prayers of your heretic son cannot have any weight, but they will be made with a full heart.[7]

For Elisabeth, to be in Lourdes was perhaps the happiest time of her life. She blossomed in the atmosphere of fervent faith and the delicate care shown to the sick. She wrote to her mother:

> Don't torment yourself about my health, it is much better than when we set off; the good air, wonderfully pure, of Lourdes, and the palpable joy is a marvel. As for our Juliette, I don't think of her as absent, for her presence is very much in my heart and our union is complete.[8]

She must also have been heartened by Félix's attitude to everything around him. During their visit thirty years before, he could see nothing admirable there, only the commercialism, what he considered superstitious fanaticism, and the revulsion he felt from the sickness around him, despite his medical training. This time, softened by his increasing respect for the way Elisabeth was coping with her illness, his attitude turned into admiration. Although he still could not understand what was going on, it still made a strong impression on him, two experiences in particular. One day they found themselves caught up in a Benediction procession by a Spanish contingent. Félix found himself, by chance, next to a young priest, totally paralysed, lying on his bed. At the moment of Benediction, the Archbishop of Barcelona came up to the priest and gave him a special blessing, in a deeply fatherly and loving way. Félix was disgusted and appalled. How could the Archbishop give such false hope and a useless blessing in the name of religion to someone so severely disabled? How could the young man himself not be revolted, as Félix himself would have been if he had been in his position? Why should he hope for a miracle that would never happen? In his eyes it was scandalous.

Félix then lost sight of the young priest, caught up in the procession, but he returned a little later to find him. He expected to find him disappointed and confused, but to his great surprise Félix saw him totally transformed. On his face was a supreme expression of joy and peace, indefinable, supernatural, something he was at a loss to explain. He then had a thought that was totally alien to him, but which seemed to have been dredged up by his Catholic upbringing: was there not at Lourdes something inexplicable and great, a particular grace for all these sick people which gives them such joy and such serenity in spite of the deception wrought in them, when they would never be healed? For the moment, he rejected this thought as so irrational that it seemed ridiculous to him.[9]

Félix told Elisabeth about the incident, and despite her husband's rejection of anything supernatural, she was thrilled to see him so moved and confused. She had to share her joy with someone, writing to Sr Goby, whom she knew would understand:

> My husband has been deeply moved by the great sights of Lourdes. I have been praying ardently to the Holy Virgin for his conversion and I have been asking her fervently for a special gift from the Sacred Heart, by the end of this month.[10]

It was Elisabeth herself who provided another occasion that deeply unnerved him, when he came across her at prayer before the Grotto. He did not want to disturb her in her prayer, so he sat there and observed her. He was unable to drag his eyes away from his wife; the sight of her was so ravishing, he wrote later, she was almost in ecstasy. Even his atheist soul could sense that there was something deeply supernatural at work there.

They returned to Paris, Félix deeply unsettled by what he had seen in his wife and in the young priest; although the memory faded, it had done something in his spirit that would bear fruit in due time.

Towards the end of July they went on their usual holiday to Jougne, but they stayed for a few days in Dijon to see Sr Goby. The Sister was attending a clinic there as she was having tests for an increasing eye trouble. Sr Goby ate with them, then in the afternoon they took trips together in the car to places around Dijon. It was during one of these excursions that Elisabeth told Sr Goby of premonitions she had had, and which she had mentioned in her letters to the Sister, that she would die young, but also that Félix would return to the practice of his faith; not only that, but he would enter the religious life. These were amazing premonitions, but not unconnected. Elisabeth had given her life, her prayer, her suffering, for the Church, for souls, but above all for her husband. She might have been encouraged by his gradual softening towards her faith and be confident that he might one day return to his Catholic roots. But it was surely a supernatural assurance from God that this would take him both into the religious life and the priesthood, which was far beyond what could be expected.

When Elisabeth and Sr Goby said farewell to each other at the station they promised to do the same thing the following year, but this was not to be.

From Jougne, Elisabeth took a few moments of 'little recreation' to write to Sr Goby, in between their settling in and setting up the household there again, as always her heart set on greater things. Her one aim, even among the mundane household chores, was to love her beloved Master more and more, to give all to him to his greater glory; she wrote:

> Let us abandon ourselves to him, and through all aridity, sadness of soul, through all the pains of heart and of life, through all bodily suffering, let us march towards the divine Light, which hides itself here below only in order to give us greater light above. Let us wrap ourselves in serenity, let us spend ourselves lavishly in charity, and let us be by prayer and sorrow apostles of Jesus. It is a beautiful programme; you will accomplish it more quickly than I.[11]

Elisabeth's health held up, they had friends to stay with them, as well as family. They ended their time in Jougne by travelling through the Italian lakes.

At the beginning of September Sr Goby wrote that she was staying in Savigny-lés-Beaune with her mother, who had become seriously ill, but by November she gave Elisabeth the good news that her mother was out of danger. She was very frail, Sr Goby wrote, but since she had feared that her mother would die, although the road would be long to a good recovery, she was very grateful. However, the fact that she would need to be with her mother for some time to come, and that her failing eyesight made her feel she might not be able to carry out her nursing duties at the Hôtel-Dieu, brought on a severe crisis of conscience about her religious vocation.

Unlike most religious Orders the sisters of the Hôtel-Dieu had considerable personal freedom—it was unusual at that time, for example, that she was able to go on an annual pilgrimage with her mother. They kept control of their own financial affairs and could leave the Order freely, without a dispensation. The letter that Sr Goby wrote to Elisabeth telling her of her anguish is the only one that Sr Goby would not allow to be published, so there is only Elisabeth's reply to it. That Sr Goby turned to Elisabeth, a lay woman, rather than to her superiors or a priest tells much of the close and intimate relationship the two women had in their spiritual lives. Elisabeth drew on her own experience to advise her:

> I want to tell you of my tender compassion in the unhappy crisis that is passing in your poor heart; I understand it and discern it in its depths. But even if the flood of suffering and bitterness is violent, don't allow it to overwhelm you; above all, under the sway of wholly natural physical and moral depression following such a shock, don't let the harmful imagination, weakening thoughts, invade your soul.[12]

She reminds the sister of the choice she made of the religious life and asks her to consider whether an alternative way would be better. They are both called to the way of suffering, she wrote, and she knows from her own experience the depths of love one has for one's mother that was partly the cause of the sister's dilemma.

Calmed by Elisabeth's long letter and heartened by her assurance of prayer, Sr Goby returned in due course to her community and her work there.

Suffering Accepted and Offered

Writing to her in the New Year 1913, Elisabeth asked her to pray for three special graces—the conversion of her husband, her mother's sanctification and a happy announcement about her niece Marie. The family had noticed the attachment that was growing between Marie and Maurice, son of their great friends the Hennequins, and on 22 May the announcement of their engagement was duly made. Elisabeth was doubly delighted, because Maurice and his family were practicing Catholics. Maurice was shortly to finish his studies at the Polytechnic School and take up a military career, and he was taken fully into the family circle. Sadly, Elisabeth did not live to see them happily married.

Elisabeth's health still held at the turn of the year but in February and March it took a severe turn for the worse. She was confined to her bed for some weeks, with continual vomiting giving her severe headaches. Her doctors gave her medicine that seemed to work, and by April she was up and about again, valiant, active and full of energy. Everyone hoped that she was fully recovered from her cancer.

In June, Félix and Elisabeth went to the great Exhibition of Gand, as Félix had to take part in jury service there. Elisabeth suffered from fatigue, and when they returned to Paris this fatigue intensified. She was bedridden for a while with vomiting, vertigo and headaches, but they gradually subsided and by July it was hoped that they could go to Jougne as usual. The rest of the family had already left Paris and Elisabeth wrote to her mother on the 25th:

> This morning I'm going to set out for the best of all visits; I have been able to go to Confession and Communion, with such great joy, because for nineteen days I have been like a plant without water. Here I am with a good supply of energy and a renewal of

> graces which enable me to bear my maladies, miseries and separations of various kinds.[13]

Six days later, on their wedding anniversary, 31 July, she wrote again to her mother:

> It is 24 years ago today; I was most radiant and most young. This morning I have received Communion in bed and I thank God for all the joys and all the graces he has given me during these years; I have prayed for all those most dear to me.[14]

In the latter part of July she felt much better and they all thought that this meant her real return to health. Both Félix and her doctors considered that the fresh air of the mountains around Jougne would speed her convalescence, so they arranged for all the domestic servants to go ahead to Jougne and make all the preparations for the summer break there. Some good friends called on the Leseurs before their departure and invited them to break the long journey to Jougne and stay with them for a few days in Sèvres.

They began their journey 1 August, and Elisabeth wrote to her mother that day:

> My bags are packed under my directions, about my bed; the servants were so helpful, and Marie [her maid] has been very stretched; but everything is so long and difficult because one is not able to move … this morning, I was helped into the car by M- who led me quite sweetly as far as the platform of B… I am installed on the ground floor, with a large open window at my side, the light on the lawns and a lovely sun. I am stretched out on a chaise-longue which is a true bed … my dinner was brought to me on the chaise-longue. Félix has returned to Paris to wind up his affairs and begins his holidays this evening. The servants leave this evening at 10.50 (a new train for Jougne). Félix is persuaded

that I won't be able to go to Jougne this Thursday; but we will be there in a few days, if I don't have any further hitches. I just need to gain enough strength to enable me to go on the train.[15]

Unfortunately, she was never able to make the journey. The first few days spent in Sèvres were good, but suddenly all her symptoms returned even more strongly, and after a week or so she was really sick. Under these conditions the Leseurs felt they could no longer stay with their friends and presume on their generous hospitality, and in any case, they, too, were due to leave to take the waters at one of the spas.

The situation was complicated; their Paris apartment was closed for the summer, all the servants were in Jougne so it would be impossible for them to return there. Even more, Elisabeth needed to be somewhere where there was expert and constant care. Félix therefore contacted the clinic on the rue de la Pompe where she had had her operation the previous year. Félix stressed that she would not be there for an operation but the illness would be serious and probably long. The clinic gladly accepted them both, because Félix did not want to be parted from her, and on 9 August they were taken to the clinic by ambulance. In fact, this arrangement was excellent, because it meant that Elisabeth would be given the care she needed, and in surroundings that she knew and loved from her previous stay there.

There was an even greater blessing awaiting her there. Her usual confessor, Fr Hébert was away, and a friend recommended a Redemptorist father of great piety, Fr Voinot, so Félix went to ask him if he would visit his wife. Fr Voinot was only too happy to do so, and he visited Elisabeth regularly for Confession and Holy Communion throughout their stay at the clinic. The benefit was on both sides. Fr Voinot never forgot meeting Elisabeth and was profoundly inspired by her submission to the will of God and her total acceptance of her suffering.

On 20 August her condition worsened, she was unable to keep food down, crises succeeded each other, she was so enfeebled that she lapsed into a sort of coma. Her doctor, Professor Guillain, did not hide the severity of her condition, and on the 27th Félix considered that she was entering into her final agony and that he was going to lose her.

Then, against all expectations, between the 2nd and 3rd September, Elisabeth suddenly turned the corner and her condition improved somewhat. There was perhaps a reason for this. When Elisabeth thought that she was getting worse, around 20 September, she had begun a novena to St Thérèse of Lisieux, for whom she had a great devotion, but whom Félix mocked, saying that 'she is childish, that little sister, she's nothing at all'.

'On the contrary, she is very great,' Elisabeth would reply to his comments, 'but you cannot understand, you cannot understand'. The change in her condition occurred at the end of the novena.

In the middle of September she was well enough to write a long letter to her mother, written in pencil because she was not strong enough to manage pen and ink, describing her illness but also her rapid recovery. She described the little altar that had been erected in her room, from where she would receive Holy Communion:

> I have truly experienced the profound power of Communion and the divine goodness in the absence of any sensible impression, or any consolation. Without God, this trial would have been very difficult for me to bear. Without God, and also, in the human sphere, without Félix. You can't imagine, dear mother, what he has meant to me. I could never forget him, and it is also for him that

> I want to look after myself, so that I can try to give him some years of tranquillity.[16]

By 18 September she was well enough to be taken by ambulance to a convalescent home run by the Franciscans on the rue de Maurepas, in Versailles, not without regret at leaving the rue de la Pompe which had looked after her so well. The Franciscans, though, had a large garden where she could sit out, take short walks and receive a few visits from family and her closest friends. Nevertheless, she was soon longing to be back home again, in familiar surroundings and with her own things around her, and they left for home on the 28th. She rested for a few days after their return and then rapidly made a remarkable recovery. She was soon able to take walks in the Champs-Elysées and the Bois de Boulogne, conveniently close to their home. She even began to take up some of her work, to write and to take part in all her usual occupations.

She didn't seem to have any pain and she was enjoying a health she had not had for several years. She enjoyed this well-being for five weeks, but then on 13 November, her fatigue returned and with it all her former symptoms. Nevertheless, by Christmas, she wrote to her mother that she was hoping to receive Communion that Friday. One of the most difficult deprivations for her was that due to her frequent vomiting she was sometimes unable to receive Communion. By New Year's Day she was well enough to receive visits from her family and close friends, and by the middle of the month she was almost back to her old self. During February, the weather was so pleasant that they were able to take car drives and short walks in the Bois de Boulogne.

Although she was able to send her last, short note to Sr Goby, the last entry in her diary was 9 January. Remarking on her severe pain, she added:

> Oh, so long as it is the divine response to me—is it not so, Lord? And so long as no least part of my pain is lost! Stronger than my poor action, stronger than my imperfect prayer, may it reach Your Heart and become the most efficacious form of supplication.[17]

Her pain and the humiliations of her illness had become her prayer, and as always, looking beyond herself, and with her deep and tender love for her family, she wished 'great and Christian love' for them all and above all their sanctification. Then she made her final prayer for herself, and the one she loved most of all, her beloved Félix:

> Unite with my soul the souls of those I love, the soul I love best of all, and put an end to this grievous solitude of spirit, which weighs on me so much. And then, sanctify me, too, by this suffering, bring me close to Your Heart and teach me to love and serve You better. I resolve (imploring divine grace) in the future to give way no more to the lapses I have known in hours of extreme pain, to be always gentle, humble, full of charity.
>
> Help me, dear Saviour.[18]

During this time of crises and periods of calm Félix kept detailed notes of her condition. He also wrote a card to Sr Goby to let her know of Elisabeth's health. Letters between the two became fewer, as Elisabeth could now only write with a pencil, and Sr Goby's eyesight meant that she could no longer write long letters. Félix, who had a deep respect for the nun, had seen how precious the friendship was between the two women, and often saw Elisabeth take out her friend's letters to read them over once more, gaining comfort and strength from them.

Gradually, Elisabeth's condition worsened, and with a doctor's understanding Félix knew that she did not have long to live. His devotion to his beloved wife was inexhaustible. He had unavoidably to leave their apartment to attend to his business, always worried while out and spending as little time as possible away from her side. He was anxious while away from her, but as soon as he was at her bedside again, he experienced a deep calm and peace, for which he could not account, and on which he pondered with astonishment. It gradually dawned on him that it was Elisabeth's own spirit that was affecting him and everyone else who came into contact with her. It was her own deep union with God, and her utter surrender to God's will; even at this juncture he realised that this had something supernatural about it. He saw that there was a gentleness of spirit about her, and once the crises had passed, she was once again her valiant and smiling self, with the same equanimity that had always characterised her. During those crises when she would be crying in pain, she would utter short prayers to Our Lady, changing slightly the familiar Catholic prayer beginning, 'O Mary, conceived without sin', adding, 'have pity on us, on me!' Even in extreme pain, her prayers and sufferings were for others first and only then for herself.

Towards the end of April, their close friend, Mme Vimont, whom Elisabeth had encouraged in her search for God, offered to share with Félix the task of keeping watch by Elisabeth's bedside, because juggling his care of Elisabeth with his business commitments had left him greatly fatigued. Even when she was totally exhausted by her suffering, Elisabeth was still thinking of others. She had a small bell by which she could summon Félix or Mme Vimont, but one night they went in to find her prostrated by a crisis without her ringing for them. Seeing an instinctive movement in Félix which she interpreted as anger, but which was his sense of sadness, she said plaintively, 'Are you angry?' He hastened to assure her that he was not, and it was with difficulty that he and her friend restrained their tears in front of her, that she should think they could ever be angry with her. He could never forget how, one day, she held out her arms to him with a smile of unutterable tenderness.

Tuesday, 28 April, a priest came from Saint-Pierre de Chaillot to give her extreme unction. The following day, as so often happens after receiving the sacrament, she rallied a little and had a last period of lucidity; she gave her beloved husband one last smile of such tenderness which almost broke his heart. She then slipped into a final period of agonising fever and thirst, which they tried to alleviate by wetting her lips with a water-filled sponge. Finally, at 10 o'clock in the morning, Sunday 3 May 1914, Feast of the Finding of the Holy Cross, when so many Masses were being celebrated around the city, in the arms of her husband she gently gave up her soul to the God whom she had loved so passionately here on earth.

Notes

[1] E. Leseur, *Lettres Sur La Souffrance* (Paris: Les Éditions du Cerf, 2012), p. 67.
[2] *Ibid.*, p. 90.
[3] E. Leseur, *My Spirit Rejoices* (Manchester, New Hampshire: Sophia Institute Press, 1996), p. 169.
[4] *Ibid.*, p. 170.
[5] *Ibid.*, p. 171.
[6] E. Leseur, *Lettres Sur La Souffrance*, p. 111.
[7] B. Chovelon, *Elisabeth et Felix Leseur* (Paris: Groupe Artège, 2015), pp. 218, 219.
[8] R. P. M.-A. Leseur (Félix Leseur), *Vie d'Elisabeth Leseur* (Paris: J. de Gigord, Editeur, 1946), p. 202.
[9] *Ibid.*, p. 220.
[10] E. Leseur, *Lettres Sur La Souffrance*, p. 156.
[11] *Ibid.*, p. 162.

[12] *Ibid.*, p. 185.
[13] M.-A. Leseur, *Vie d'Elisabeth Leseur,* p. 332.
[14] *Ibid.*
[15] *Ibid.*, p. 333.
[16] *Ibid.*, p. 337ff.
[17] E. Leseur, *My Spirit Rejoices*, p. 193.
[18] *Ibid.*, p. 104.

11

FÉLIX'S CONVERSION

I N THE DIARY he kept, Félix wrote, 3 May:

> She has been installed on her deathbed, and the expression of suffering that she had in the morning has been succeeded by a ravishing expression of bliss, an exquisite smile. A gentle vision and very consoling to retain.[1]

The 'look of immortal beauty' as Félix described it, Elisabeth's face bearing the calm of another world, moved him deeply. The nurse who, during her illness, had helped care for Elisabeth, was equally struck by the beauty of her expression, saying over and over to Félix 'Mme Leseur has suffered a lot', and noted that her face had borne an almost supernatural expression, even when she had been in a coma.

The following day he wrote, 'The same expression of a being rejoicing and of a supernatural peace. She is wonderful and lovely to contemplate.' Their painter friend Duvent came in the evening to make a sketch of her, and Félix was still wondering whether there was something above the mundane there.

Another thing that amazed him was the number of people who came to pay their respects to Elisabeth on her bier. Besides their many mutual friends, there were many unknown to him, whom he had never seen before and who he would never see again, of obviously modest means for the most part. Their sorrow was evident, as was their respect for Elisabeth. These were the people for whom she had done so much, giving generously of her time and her resources, spiritual and material, and they were there now to show their gratitude. It gave Félix a small insight into the hidden charity she had practised all her life.

The feeling of something supernatural around Elisabeth was with him during the Requiem Mass that was held in her own parish church of Saint-Pierre de Chaillot two days later, and—still an atheist!—he had a real sense of the communion of saints that transcends earthly life. The priests who assisted at the Mass were amazed at the number of people who crowded into the church, saying that never before had they seen such crowds at a Requiem Mass. The anguish that her mother felt, losing her third daughter, can be imagined, but perhaps the reverence shown for Elisabeth was of some comfort to her.

Nonetheless, in the days following, Félix was devastated by his loss and nothing could comfort him. With his world collapsing around him he began sorting through Elisabeth's effects and came across the *Spiritual Testament* she had written out for him as far back as 15 October 1905.[2]

Addressed to 'my beloved husband', it is a remarkable document that rings with the certainty that Félix would indeed return to the Faith, and that he would carry on her work of prayer and service. In this she wanted him to be 'my chief and dearest heir'. She left to him, and to all who loved her 'the task of praying', and 'as far as a poor human creature can, my immense debt of gratitude to the adored Father, whom you shall know and love through my prayers in heaven'.

She wanted him to carry on her loving oversight of their nephews and nieces who meant so much to her; also the building of a chapel, begun by Juliette with small gifts of money she received at Easter and Christmas, and which Elisabeth continued:

> And now, my beloved Félix, I tell you once more
> of my great love. And I charge you to tell our

> relatives and friends how much I loved them all and how much I shall pray for them until the hour of reunion. Close to God, where other dear ones already await us, we shall one day be eternally reunited. I hope for this through all my afflictions offered for you and through divine mercy.[3]

In these few words Elisabeth summed up the whole meaning of her life of love and suffering, and her supreme confidence in the Communion of Saints.

Félix read this Testament over and over and, encouraged by Amélie, who knew of its existence, her Diary. This completely overwhelmed him. It filled the void in his life; he read there of the immense love his wife had had for him and the prayer and suffering she offered for him. He was overcome, also, by remorse that for so many years he had opposed and ridiculed his wife for a faith that he now saw had sustained her throughout her illnesses and that had mattered so deeply to her. He was at first struck on a superficial level by the depth of her thought, the beauty of her style and the ardent charity evident on every page. But as he read it over and over, it was her faith that captivated him more and more. He felt guided by Elisabeth herself, drawing him gently but firmly into her own world vision of the realities of the supernatural, against all his natural inclinations as an atheist.

In the account he wrote of his conversion Félix stressed that this was not due to his 'intellectual side':

> I was not affected by study or reading or exegesis or apologetics or theological knowledge, for, in fact, I possessed none. I was at the time versed in all the doctrines of rationalism, which are radically opposed to Catholicism.[4]

All these studies of Catholicism could, of course, bring someone to faith; although the Church is opposed to rationalism, that is, the belief that only what can be proved by rational means is to be believed, it is not opposed to rational thinking about the faith: faith and reason are two God-given faculties we possess; they complement but are never in opposition.

It is evidence of the divine sense of humour that Félix would be brought back to the faith by the precise aspects of being human that transcend human thought, which as an atheist he most despised, to which he had refused to give credence and had labelled as superstition.

After Elisabeth's death, and as he recovered slightly from his bereavement, he returned 'to live in the midst of people hostile or indifferent not only to religion but to everything spiritual'. It was, he said, that in this practically atheistic atmosphere that 'I first heard God's voice and began to be illumined by His light'.

That journey had already begun by what he had observed of his wife during her illness, and what he had seen of her on her deathbed, with that almost supernatural aura surrounding her; he now felt a natural revulsion against materialism, and like so many before and after questioned whether:

> it was possible that such splendid qualities, such intelligence, so many virtues and aspirations, so much self-denial and self-sacrifice could be so suddenly annihilated. If it were indeed possible, then all that constitutes the beauty of any existence would be a mere illusion, and every noble effort would be useless, because nothing remains after we have passed away.[5]

He was so horrified at himself for having such thoughts, so inimical to a staunch atheist such as himself, that he deliberately tried to harden his heart against them. It was incomprehensible to him, as he read Elisabeth's diary, that anyone could have such an intense love for One whom he believed was 'merely an abstract entity, a concept of the human imagination'.

The only consolation for him at this point was that he was beginning to know, understand and love the real Elisabeth for the first time and draw some consolation from reading her diary.

A few weeks after the funeral a close friend, whom Félix described as not at all religious, and quite indifferent to the Faith, Léon Mahuet, suggested that they should go away together, to get some fresh air and a change of scenery. Félix was grateful for the invitation but at the same time reluctant to leave the apartment which carried so many memories; also, that he would not be able to make his daily visits to Elisabeth's grave in the cemetery at Montmartre.

Léon eventually persuaded him, and they left Paris 9 June. They were driving from Uzerche to Tulle, through a forest of beautiful chestnut trees and Félix was enjoying the drive, the beauty of the countryside and the fresh air and brightness of which he had deprived himself for so long. Suddenly, out of the blue, he remembered a conversation he had had with Elisabeth the previous year, and heard her repeat a phrase with which she had begun their conversation: 'I am grieved'. That first time he knew it referred to him—to his atheism—and he said she had uttered it with the greatest affection 'and in a most touching tone of supplication'. He now heard it once again, but with a different emphasis, and he was overcome by emotion. It was as if Elisabeth was in the car with them. The thought then came to him, and changed his whole being, 'if Elisabeth is alive—and what I have just witnessed convinces me that she is—it is because the soul is immortal, because there is a God, and because the existence of the supernatural is a philosophical truth'.[6]

This did indeed erode what he had thought of as the firmest of foundations in his atheist belief, that there is no such thing as a soul, that there is no life after death, that there is no God. He was brought, however dimly, to this conclusion, not by his reason or by any external proof, but by what he would have dismissed as pure human emotion or even delusion in another. He felt that there was present a force external to himself acting upon him, and this apprehension was so real, so powerful, that he could not dismiss it.

They arrived at Rocamadour in the afternoon, and once again under an uncontrollable impulse, in the church he bought a taper and lit it before the altar for Elisabeth's intention, an action that before he had always dismissed as superstition.

They made their way back to Paris five days later, and Félix asked if they could return by way of places that had been dear to his wife. Their first stop was at Paray-le-Monial, which, because of her devotion to the Sacred Heart, had been very dear to Elisabeth.

At first, Félix was not impressed with the small church and town; he went into the Cluniac Basilica, where at least he could admire its architecture, but Elisabeth had more in mind for him than that. As he was walking around the choir he once again sensed her presence even more strongly than before and he knelt in prayer for a quarter of an hour. He did not know what prayer to say but simply asked Elisabeth to pray for him.

He also kept a promise he had made to Elisabeth some time ago, but which he was unable to fulfil during her life. Now, their travels took them close to Chateaugay where Mamie, their elderly servant lived, and who was now retired. She was able to bring the first smile to his face as she recounted stories of her time with the Arrighi family and anecdotes of her 'great love', Elisabeth, as she was growing up.

They also stopped off at Beaune, where he visited Sr Goby. He had already been impressed by her, and respected her, but now he would visit her regularly. He developed a deep friendship with her until her death in 1922, deeply loved by her sisters in Beaune and the wider community, as well as the many patients she had nursed so faithfully. Many soldiers also came to her funeral, because during the First World War the Hospital had been opened up to receive the wounded.

Back in Paris, the experiences he had had faded somewhat as he took up his ordinary life and work again, while doing his best to dismiss the impression they had made on him. It was easier and more comfortable to revert to his old habits of thought and scepticism. Three weeks later he spent ten days in Rheims, his native town, with one of his oldest friends. This friend and his wife were ardent Catholics and so he was immersed into an ordinary Catholic family life where faith took completely naturally the dominant place in the household. One afternoon he sat with the wife and she helped him to express his grief, revealing her own deep faith with complete simplicity. He recognised in her the same high moral sense that had been so pronounced in Elisabeth, a sense that sprung solely from their faith, living examples of Christianity in practice. All the supernatural milieu that he had lived in at Tulle and Paray-le-Monial resurfaced, and he returned to Paris a little closer to accepting what he had experienced there.

However, external events were beginning to crowd in, with the immanent prospect of war. Being in such close contact with people from the worlds of politics, government and the press, Félix would have been even better informed of it than most. His brother-in-law and three of their nephews joined the French army, and for a while in August 1914 there seemed to be some success on the French side. With the retreat from Belgium and the German advance towards Paris things took a turn for the worse. On 25 August the board of directors of the Insurance Company of which Félix was manager, asked him to take the funds of the company into safe keeping in Bordeaux. He therefore ordered a car for the 31st to take him and his secretary, but the day before panic had set in in Paris and the car was no longer available. Everybody was trying to leave the city by whatever means possible.

Félix went to the garage owner's house and met there a gentleman who was also preparing to leave for Bordeaux with a friend, in a powerful car he had been lent. They offered to share it with Félix and his companion, and he gratefully accepted. They travelled as far as Orléans, which was crowded with people, and at first the chauffeur refused to take them any further; having persuaded him to take them as far as Vierzon, which was less crowded, they parted company, with Félix and his secretary taking the train to Bordeaux. It was so crowded that they were forced to travel in the luggage van, while keeping an eye on their precious portmanteau carrying the company's assets.

Sitting on the box, exhausted and yet grateful for how everything had worked out for them, Félix once again heard an inner voice:

> You were able to leave Paris in a most unexpected, almost miraculous manner, but do not think that this was simply in order to safeguard the material interests entrusted to your care. That was only incidental: the true reason and aim of all this is your innermost being, which is here in question; it was necessary that you should be enabled to go to

Lourdes, where God is awaiting you; Lourdes is the real object of your present journey. Go to Lourdes.[7]

Félix at first questioned whether he was dreaming, given his fatigue, but he was wide awake, although fighting against this inner voice. The command was repeated, with increasing urgency, and taking on the sound of Elisabeth's voice until a sort of light shone in his mind. Once again, he could no longer resist the divine command, and agreed that as soon as he had finished his work in Bordeaux he would go to Lourdes.

It was not easy to complete his mission in Bordeaux, which like every other major city was crammed with people, and which a few days later, with the fall of Paris, became the seat of government. He therefore spent his time going to the various churches there, praying, while he was still battling with his atheistic rationalism which tempted him to see all his experiences as coming from a fevered imagination. But gradually that inner resistance was giving way to faith.

Once he was free to leave Bordeaux, Félix went to spend a few days of rest with a very close family friend, in the valley of the Garonne, near Marmande. She was a widow, with two daughters living with her. He described her as 'a woman of remarkable intelligence and distinction and of exceptionally high moral character, which was enhanced by her simplicity and sincerity'.[8] The daughters staying with her were of a similar character. As well, they were devout Catholics, living out their faith with all those characteristics of simplicity, sincerity and intelligence.

Félix found that he was able to open himself out fully to this dear friend, telling another person for the first time of his inner searching, of his doubts and hopes, and always there was the spirit of Elisabeth among them. Félix read aloud from her diary, which delighted and moved the three women. After a few days, Félix felt himself refreshed enough in spirit to make his fateful journey to Lourdes.

He found the town much changed from his previous visits because very few pilgrims were making their way to it, and there were no religious processions or crowds. Instead, the hospices had been put at the disposal of the military to nurse the wounded. Lourdes had changed for him in a much deeper way as well, as he recalled the first time that he had come, despising and mocking what he perceived as the superstition, the gullibility, the 'fraudulent cures', the commercialism of it all. But he also recalled their last visit when he had seen Elisabeth in an ecstasy of prayer before the Grotto, and it was her spirit, above all that was with him now.

One morning, he made his way to the Grotto and dropped to his knees in fervent prayer, praying for the gift of faith. He went there every day and gradually he felt his heart changing:

> Now my eyes were being opened, and I began to perceive that the Grotto of Massabielle is a sacred place, where God does indeed reveal Himself, and grace flows abundantly. I felt at peace within myself, and my sorrow began to assume a fresh meaning, in accordance with Elisabeth's profound words: 'Suffering gives birth to life'. I thanked God with all my heart. Of course, my faith was not yet self-conscious and reasoned, but henceforth I felt myself turning towards it, and was sure that I should find it and enter upon a new existence.[9]

Lourdes, which as an atheist he despised, was precisely the place where his heart was changed and he returned to Paris a new man. He believed, but his faith now had to seek understanding. He began reading from Elisabeth's substantial library of religious and theological books, which he also catalogued. He began attending Sunday Mass, appreciating the beauty of it, and knowing that he was pleasing Elisabeth. He also began reading the Gospels, which so captivated him now that they became his essential daily reading. By March 1915 he decided he needed to go to a priest and be reconciled to the Church, but old habits and human respect held him back. He went to his parish priest, a holy man and highly educated, who welcomed him and listened carefully to his story, but he still could not make up his mind to go to Confession, although another part of him knew it would be inevitable.

There was an old friend of his who had gone through a conversion experience very much like his own, and Félix was able to speak freely to him of his doubts and fears. Walking home from a party together at the end of March the friend asked him how he was getting on. Two days later he came to see Félix and said that he had made an appointment with a very good priest who would help him through his Confession. With an appointment made for the 30th, Félix had no option now than to take the next step. The priest was none other than Elisabeth's former director, Fr Hébert.

He was now ready to make his confession, and then, Fr. Hébert having absolved him, said to him, 'Tomorrow you will go to Communion'. Félix was taken aback and replied, 'What, my father, just like that, so quickly?'

'Yes, you will receive Communion tomorrow.'[10]

Félix left the church overcome with intense joy at his return to God, with his inner peace restored. He decided to go to Mass the following day in the chapel next to their apartment, and to which Elisabeth herself had gone regularly. He felt her presence very near to him as he received the sacred Host for the first time after so many years, but returning home after Mass all his old prejudices and cynicism returned. He told himself that he didn't have proof, apart from his own expectations, and that there was nothing positive or objective in what he had just done.

He persuaded himself that he was a victim of his imagination and of auto-suggestion, a real fool, and asked himself, then, that in such circumstances why he should continue in this new way of life. He was grieving and conflicted; as at this time he went every morning to Elisabeth's grave, he took as usual the Metro to Montmartre cemetery.

Waiting for the train, sitting on the bench alone and despairing, thinking over all that had happened, he decided not to continue the religious practices he had just begun. Then, just as everything seemed to collapse around him he once again heard an interior voice, Elisabeth's voice, saying to him:

> But that would be too convenient! If, after having all your life as a man renounced and battled against God and Jesus Christ, when you have confessed and received Communion and you go to possess straight away all the clarity, all the consolations, this would be almost immoral. It is no longer a question of going by your feelings but by your will; from now on you must put yourself at the service of Jesus Christ, to truly win faith by grace.[11]

This was so truly the voice of Elisabeth that he was overwhelmed and felt he had found the truth. By the time he reached her grave he was completely won over, his mind was clear. He determined to go to Communion the following day, and from then on he never looked back.

With these undeniable impressions of a living Elisabeth, Félix was being introduced to the doctrine of the Communion of Saints that had played such a central role in his wife's spirituality. Writing to their friends the Duvents

Félix's Conversion

some three years before, after the death of their son, Elisabeth explained what was, and what was not meant by this doctrine. It seems that the Duvents, in their grief, might have been dabbling in spiritualism:

> Indeed, yes, there are in the supernatural order many things surprising to our poor reason; but what is admirable in Catholicism is that it upholds, despite everything, the rights of reason and never permits this unpleasant blend of materialism and spiritual things which is so shocking in spiritualism. It is not by making these 'invocations', in trying to call forth these 'appearances' in which it is easy to see the danger, that we are united with our departed loved ones.
>
> It is, rather, in coming to God by prayer and charity, in each day lifting our soul more and more towards the light and divine truth, in doing our best to become better people, more conformed to the Gospel ideal. And then we come to perceive ourselves very close to these dear souls who are living in the heart of this truth, of this love, this holiness that we ourselves are striving to know and to attain.
>
> It is after Communion, in the happy recollection of thanksgiving after Mass, that I find myself in intimate union with the souls that I loved so deeply here below, whom I love and who love me forever.[12]

By the July of 1915, Félix had become completely convinced for himself of the Communion of Saints. He was planning to stay as usual in Jougne, but friends who lived there were thinking that perhaps it might be too much of an ordeal for him to be in a place which Elisabeth had loved so much and which held so many memories for him. He wrote to them on the 20th to reassure them; he showed how much the doctrine of the Communion of Saints had changed him and which was now so important to him, too:

> I am counting on leaving for Jougne about the 25th or 26th, or at least by the end of the month. How I'm longing for this stay in Jougne! I'm longing for it with all my heart, and I'm being slow in being able to carry it out. Evidently, it will be a very emotional time for me at the beginning, when I'll find myself alone in that countryside and in that house, which I love so much. But afterwards, what a sweet retreat there will be in my sentiments and my memories! I will not be alone morally. She will be close to me even more than in Paris. More than that, my dear friend, I am even more convinced that the dead are the ones who are truly alive, who are in the light and in the fullness of life, and that they are close to us, guiding us and surrounding us. It is what the Catholic Church calls the Communion of Saints, and I know of nothing more consoling, more peaceful, than this conviction. I am living constantly with Bébeth, near to her, and I prefer to seek out those places where she is most present and that she loved. It is to tell you that my stay in Jougne will be for me of the utmost sweetness.[13]

Her Diary had been so beneficial to him that he began to think of publishing it. Already friends were anxious for him to do so and were also anxious to read it. He therefore asked Fr Hébert to read it, which he did. Handing it back to him the priest said it was a work of great beauty, but above all it was 'the clear and solid reasoning, the gospel-like vitality, and above all the soundness of doctrine' that so impressed him.[14] He said that it should definitely be published and suggested, also, that Félix should write an introduction to it. It was Elisabeth's 'soundness of doctrine' that had always impressed Fr Hébert, as he had told him in a conversation a few days before, so with this endorsement Félix went ahead with the publication.

It was published in 1917 and sales soon topped 100,000 copies; it was swiftly translated into several languages. All this happened during the First World War and helped many to see some sense in that senseless slaughter. This was something that Elisabeth had foreseen. Six days before her death, her sister Amélie had been sitting by her bedside when Elisabeth

> suddenly woke up. With an expression of keen anxiety and with great feeling she said, 'We must pray, we must pray a great deal!'
>
> 'But, dearest, we do pray,' Amélie replied, 'we pray a great deal for you.'
>
> 'No,' Elisabeth replied with the same intense feeling, 'that is not what I mean: we must pray for all those wounded, for all those poor wounded.'
>
> 'But what wounded? There aren't any.'
>
> 'Yes, yes! We must pray for them, pray a great deal.' And then her face continued to express the same anxious pity.[15]

Elisabeth was spared the anguish of seeing her beloved France so devastated, as well as such slaughter, but there is no doubt God gave her a prophetic insight into it and made her suffering part of her prayer for it. So many found help and solace in reading her Diary during this time, especially soldiers who needed to make some sense of what they were going through. Spreading the message of Elisabeth and her heroic life would henceforth be Félix's life work.

Notes

[1] R. P. M.-A. Leseur (Félix Leseur), *Vie d'Elisabeth Leseur* (Paris: J. de Gigord, Editeur, 1946), p. 351.
[2] E. Leseur, *My Spirit Rejoices* (Manchester: New Hampshire: Sophia Institute Press, 1996), pp. 197ff.
[3] *Ibid.*, p. 199.
[4] E. Leseur, *Light in the Darkness* (Manchester, New Hampshire: Sophia Institute Press, 1998), p. 7.
[5] *Ibid.*, p. 9.
[6] *Ibid.*, p. 12.
[7] *Ibid.*, p. 19.
[8] *Ibid.*, p. 20.
[9] *Ibid.*, p. 23.
[10] M.-A. Leseur, *Vie d'Elisabeth Leseur*, p. 353.
[11] *Ibid.*, p. 354.
[12] *Ibid.*, pp. 326ff.
[13] *Ibid.*, pp. 328ff.
[14] E. Leseur, *My Spirit Rejoices*, p. 35.
[15] *Ibid.*, p. 38.

12

THE PRIESTHOOD

BESIDES HIS WORK on Elisabeth's writings, there was another burning issue that occupied Félix's thoughts. Even before he had been reconciled to the Church he had thought of the priesthood, and after his conversion he was filled with a love for God that in his atheist days he would have considered meaningless. Not surprisingly, when he brought the matter up with his relatives there was total opposition. On one level, this would have been understandable, because such a profound change in him and the desire to enter the religious life, could be seen as an extreme reaction so soon after Elisabeth's death.

Nevertheless, two months after his return to the Church, on Pentecost Sunday 1915, he was received into the Third Order of the Dominicans. This meant that, as a lay person, he was a true son of the Order, living the Dominican charism in the world.

His choice of this Order might have been influenced by Fr Hébert, now his director and himself a Dominican, but it was also the ideal choice for him. The charism of the Order was that of preaching; for priests, this was of course by preaching, and for everyone, lay people, nuns and friars alike, preaching by the example of a holy life, combined with study and learning, above all, of the Scriptures. In Félix's case it would not inhibit the task that he now felt was God-given, to spread the news of Elisabeth's life and writings.

Fr Hébert might have thought that becoming a Dominican Tertiary was the limit of Félix's aims, but for Félix himself this was only the first step towards entering the First

Order as a friar. When he discussed this with his director in September, Fr Hébert was totally against it. He had practical reasons for this; there was the problem of Félix's age, which could make it difficult for him to adapt to such a different lifestyle; there was, perhaps, a 'convert's' excessive zeal and the short time after being a professed atheist for most of his life; above all, that he could do much more good in his chosen profession in the world than as a friar.

None of this deterred Félix. The calling from God was too strong to ignore, and it grew with every obstacle placed in his way. In the end, Fr Hébert could no longer ignore his persistence and the strength of his resolve, so in October 1917, Félix went with him to the Dominican College in Rome, where the priest was due to preach at a retreat preparatory to the reopening of the College. Fr Hébert had asked for an audience with the Pope, and the two of them met with him 21 October. Félix gave him a copy of Elisabeth's Diary and told the Pope of his desire to enter the Dominicans. To his surprise, the Pope was vehement in his rejection of the idea, and explained:

> No, do not think of it. Whenever I am consulted regarding a late vocation like yours, I do my best to discourage it. One ought to distrust the most generous enthusiasm. Especially at your age, after a conversion totally opposed to a whole lifetime without religion, I cannot too earnestly advise you to refrain from taking this step. Live as a fervent Catholic in the world, that will be far better from every point of view.[1]

Félix was not to be deterred and explained how he had been thinking deeply about it for some time, against almost total opposition, until he had convinced Fr Hébert that he truly had a genuine vocation. Fr Hébert also spoke out in his defence, and finally the Pope gave him his blessing: 'I bless your undertaking with all my heart'.

What the Pope did not know was that years earlier, Elisabeth herself had foreseen his vocation, saying to her husband, 'I shall die before you. And when I am dead, you will be converted; and when you are converted, you will become a religious. You will be Father Leseur.'[2]

It could be objected that, being aware of Elisabeth's prophecy, Félix felt some obligation to fulfill the prophecy, as it were, but there is no indication at all of this in his account. His desire for the priesthood came from deep within himself and, because it came from God who is outside time, Elisabeth's deep conviction, her prophecy, would indeed come about.

His friendship with Fr. Hébert was fruitful for Félix in other ways. He could enable Félix to see his wife's spiritual life from a different perspective. He knew from Elisabeth herself how deep was her longing for her husband's conversion, for the conversion of souls, but he pointed out to Félix, something that he had never thought of before, that she never pressured him into believing as she did, never 'lectured' him. Her husband perhaps did not realise how much it cost her to she remain silent when her faith was under attack. Like many atheists, he was perhaps under the impression that his arguments were far stronger than hers and that this accounted for her silence. But for Elisabeth, she felt that the witness of the joy she possessed, the quiet practice of her faith and the fruit it bore in loving charity, patience and endurance, spoke far more loudly than many words and arguments.

On the other hand Fr Hébert appreciated that Félix had put no obstacle to Elisabeth practising her faith, although Félix was honest enough to say that this really applied only to the last two years of her life, when he had dropped most of his opposition.

Félix entered the Dominican Order in 1919. Since the Order had been expelled under the Law of Associations he had to travel to Belgium and entered Le Saulchoir monastery in Kain. After a short retreat, he was clothed in the habit, taking the name of Marie-Albert. Monastic life was not an easy transition for him. He was used to fine food and wines, he was used to well-heated apartments. Now, he had to accustom himself to simple food, a hard bed and an unheated monastery. He was 58 years of age, and all the other men who entered with him were young men, often newly discharged from the military after the war. It was unsurprising, then, that shortly after entering he became seriously ill with phlebitis, and was bed-ridden for four months, thus delaying his First Profession.

In the Novitiate, because of his medical training, he was given the charge of the Novitiate infirmary. He wrote to a friend, Mme Barthou, that he felt himself to be on the fringes of the community, perhaps because of the age difference, but this was not how the other young novices viewed him. They soon came to respect his wisdom, his smile and his kindly nature; further, he brought to the Order a lifetime of experience and culture; the novices called him a living dictionary!

He made his First Profession 23 September 1920. He then began his studies for the priesthood in philosophy and theology, but the writings of Elisabeth were never far from his mind. In his cell he had a reproduction of the portrait Duvent had done of Elisabeth in 1900, and that meditative pose was an unfailing source of inspiration to him. With the encouragement of his superiors he began compiling the collection of letters to her friends which he saw published in 1922 under the title *Lettres á des Incroy-*

ants. He returned briefly to Paris to launch its publication and to meet with friends, but he was no longer M Leseur; in his white robes, now Frère Marie-Albert, he was far more at home with his brother friars than in the milieu in which he had previously moved.

He took his final vows 23 March 1923 and was ordained to the priesthood 8 July in Lille, in the church of Saint-Maurice, at the hands of the bishop of Lille, Mgr Quillet. Since the Dominicans had been allowed to return to France a short while before, he then returned to Paris and said his first Mass in the crypt of the Dominican convent in the faubourg Saint-Honoré. He could not help but recall that it was the same church, twenty years before, in which Elisabeth had stood as sponsor to the young man becoming Catholic, when Félix had been so incredulous that anyone would think of taking such a step. Now, a Dominican and a priest, he recalled that this was what Elisabeth had foretold. He testified that at these decisive moments when he received the habit, was ordained and celebrated his first Mass, he had the distinct impression of Elisabeth's presence, an impression which was almost physical, very close to him:

> It is certain that, since she is no more, she has made a Christian of me, who is striving to follow in her steps. I live with her, in thought and by prayer, much more intimately than during her life. This is not to be marvelled at, since supernatural realities are more real than anything else. Is not God the Being, in his essence, the reality *par excellance*?[3]

After his ordination Félix stayed on at the faubourg Saint-Honoré to edit, because of his previous journalistic experience, a newly established Dominican revue, *Les Nouvelles Religieuses*. He held this post for ten years, but with the publication of Elisabeth's writings he found that he was receiving more and more correspondence from those who had been inspired by her. On 14 November 1924 he gave his first conference on her in Liège, Belgium, which was to be the first of many. None gave him greater delight, though, than an invitation, the following year, from the parish priest of Jougne. He began his talk there:

> It isn't without profound emotion that I sit on this chair. Who would have said, in 1895, the year of my first visit to Jougne, that one day I would return in the white habit of Saint Dominic? It would have seemed extravagant to me, and yet it has happened. But I have not come to Jougne alone; like me, my dear Elisabeth loved Jougne and you loved her. She was solicitous for everyone; she was all goodness, wholly devoted because she was all God's and the best way of loving one's neighbour is to love God. And because of this, dear brothers, I ask for your pardon, and I ask it sincerely. For so many years, alas, I gave you a bad example, a horrid example of irreligion. How I would like to make amends for this today! Thankfully, God was merciful, as he always is. He heard Elisabeth's constant prayers that she made to him for my conversion, which she never doubted. He accepted her sacrifices, her suffering, the gift of her life that she offered to him for souls and for me. He allowed that I should be the first conquest of her posthumous apostolate which for ten years has providentially expanded through the whole world, an influence and a light which is so extraordinary that it can't be explained in human terms.[4]

Through reading her diary and other writings, but above all by his sense of her continuing presence, he had truly come to know and understand her better, because he no longer blocked out, by his atheism, what was most vital in Elisabeth's life; now, with the encouragement of his superiors, spreading her message was to become more and more his life's work. This was temporarily halted in 1932 when he became seriously ill, but even then he continued to answer the volume of mail that poured in. He wrote to each one personally. Following Elisabeth's example, he was conscious that he had to respond sensitively to that person's individual journey in the spiritual life, whether he knew them personally or no. He mentioned in one letter that he had 69 letters on his hospital table awaiting a reply.

In addition, he had another project to which he was giving a great deal of attention. On 12 August 1930, he went to stay for a holiday with a nephew near Biarritz, carrying with him the manuscript of his book *Vie d'Élisabeth Leseur*. Thus far, people had come to know Elisabeth through her published letters, diaries and assorted writings, but Félix wanted them to know her as a person and to be inspired by her holiness and her example. He also wanted to explore in more depth the main aspects of her spirituality. The book was published in December 1930 and increased even more the knowledge and appreciation of Elisabeth.

Inevitably, there were increasing calls for her beatification. With the approval of his superiors Félix began the arduous task of gathering her writings, of cataloguing the letters he received, the favours and cures attributed to her, which would be necessary to present her Cause in Rome. The first of the meetings to examine all the documentation Félix had amassed took place 30 November 1936 in the faubourg Saint-Honoré. However, shortly afterwards he became seriously ill once more which halted the process for a while. Once he had recovered, he began his journeys again, halted only in 1939 by the outbreak of the Second World War.

In 1940 he was sent to Cannes, which was more beneficial for his failing health, but his thoughts were with the terrible events overtaking his beloved country. More happily, 31 July, he recalled that he had been married to Elisabeth for 51 years—death could not come between the bonds that united them. However, he longed to return to Paris, because communication had been cut off between the two parts of the country, and in Cannes he was unable to continue working for the Cause of Elisabeth's canonisation. Undeterred, he eventually made a perilous journey back to Paris and arrived there 11 November 1942, back with his brothers and the monastic life that he loved. The following year, he managed to make another journey, this time to Besançon, in whose diocese Jougne was. He wanted to obtain from the archbishop the dossier he had on Elisabeth's cause. To his dismay, the archbishop brusquely dismissed him, saying, perhaps with good cause, that with the German Occupation he had more important matters to deal with. Félix was crushed and had to return to Paris, knowing that, without this dossier, the Cause could not be presented to Rome and its progress was now halted.

Félix had to accept this, despite all the enormous effort he had put in, and acknowledge that with his failing health and increasing age he could do no more, and that this was the will of God.

He had also to acknowledge that his mind was gradually failing him, that wonderful intellect which in his later years he had devoted unreservedly to God. The greatest sorrow was that, because of his failing memory, he was no longer able to say Mass. His superior placed him in the hospital of Perpetual Succour of Levallois. He was distraught at first at this decision because he thought he would no longer be with his community; however, there was a section reserved for the Dominicans, so he could still be with his brothers.

Later, he was moved to a small hospice for the elderly, Saint-Joseph de Chaudron-en-Mauges. Although it was a beautiful place, specially reserved for the Dominicans, the move into a new home proved to be even more unsettling for him. He became disorientated and soon after his arrival he had a fall and fractured his femur.

Even then, with his mind ever more confused, he retained, as the mother superior who ran the hospice said, his innate courtesy, never complaining, a model religious, humble and obedient.

It was impossible to operate on his leg and his decline was swift. As he received Extreme Unction he remarked: 'The good God will end well by coming to look for me. When he comes I will say to him, "Here I am!" and a few minutes later, "Eternity, what a tremendous mystery!"'[5]

He lapsed into a semi coma, and 25 February 1950 he slipped quietly away to God, the Good Shepherd, who had never ceased to search for him. His final resting place was by the side of Elisabeth, his beloved wife, who had never ceased to pray for him.

In her Spiritual Testament to him, Elisabeth wrote:

> When you also shall have become His child, the disciple of Jesus Christ and a living member of His Church, consecrate your existence, transformed by grace, to prayer and the giving of yourself in charity. Be a Christian and an apostle. All that my prayers and trials have asked for our poor brothers here below, try to give them in your turn. Love souls, pray, suffer, and work for them. They deserve all our pains, all our efforts, and all our sacrifices.[6]

Elisabeth wrote this for her husband, and there can be little doubt that he fulfilled her wishes. But it also sums up her own life and message and is a blueprint for every Christian.

Elisabeth Leseur is now Venerable Elisabeth Leseur, and the cause for her beatification and canonisation has been taken up again by the Dominican Order. Although they were divided by conflicting beliefs during their married life together, Elisabeth and Félix are an outstanding example of the depth of love in married life that could overcome all obstacles. Their lives are an example of persistent prayer and the power of divine grace to change even the hardest of hearts; their example gives hope to a world where militant secular atheism is so prevalent and married life and Christianity itself are under attack as never before, that the grace of God can prevail in the most unlikely of situations.

Prayer asking for the Intercession of Elisabeth Leseur Servant of God

God, our Father, you fortified Your servant Elisabeth with admirable prudence and a profound interior life, so that she could bear witness to Christ before her husband and in the unbelieving world that surrounded her. You gave her great meekness, making her capable of accepting her sufferings as an agreeable prayer to you.

We thank you, Father, for the gifts that You gave her, for the example she has given to the women of today, and for the benefits obtained in our family through her intercession.

We confidently beseech you that through her intercession you grant us the grace of …

(*Ask for the grace desired.*)

We also ask that, if it be Your will, the Church may recognize the holiness of Elisabeth's life, for the glory of the Holy Trinity. We ask this through Christ Our Lord. Amen.

With ecclesiastical approval

Notes

[1] E. Leseur, *Light in the Darkness* (Manchester, New Hampshire: Sophia Institute Press, 1998), p. 29.
[2] *Ibid.*, p. 30.
[3] R. P. M.-A. Leseur (Félix Leseur), *Vie d'Elisabeth Leseur* (Paris: J. de Gigord, Editeur, 1946), p. 329.
[4] B. Chovelon, *Élisabeth et Félix Leseur* (Paris: Groupe Artège, 2015), pp. 343ff.
[5] *Ibid.*, pp. 382ff.
[6] E. Leseur, *My Spirit Rejoices* (Manchester: New Hampshire: Sophia Institute Press, 1996), p. 197.

Bibliography

Chovelon, B., *Élisabeth et Félix Leseur* (Paris: Groupe Artège, 2015).

Cobban, A., *A History of Modern France Vols 2 &3* (Middlesex: Penguin, 1965).

Leseur, E., *Journal d'enfant* (Paris: Les Editions du Cerf, 2012).

Leseur, E., *Lettres á des Incroyants* (Paris: J. de Gigord, Editor, 1928).

Leseur, E., *Light in the Darkness* (Manchester, New Hampshire: Sophia Institute Press, 1998).

Leseur, E., *My Spirit Rejoices* (Manchester, New Hampshire: Sophia Institute Press, 1996).

Leseur, E., *Lettres Sur La Souffrance* (Paris: Editions du Cerf, 2012).

Leseur, F., *Vie d'Elisabeth Leseur* (Paris: J. de Gigord 1946).

Ruffing, J. K., RSM (edited, translated and introduced by), *Elisabeth Leseur* (New York: Classics of Western Spirituality, Paulist Press, 2005).